1X5/14, LT 5/13

ANCIENT MESOPOTAMIA

DR. ERICA C. D. HUNTER

THIRD EDITION

CHELSEA HOUSE
PUBLISHERS
An imprint of Infobase Publishing

Cultural Atlas for Young People
ANCIENT MESOPOTAMIA
Third Edition

Copyright © 2007 The Brown Reference Group plc

Chelsea House
An imprint of Infobase Publishing
132 West 31st Street
New York, NY 10001

Library of Congress Cataloging-in-Publication Data
available upon request.

ISBN: 0-8160-6824-0

ISBN 13 digit: 978-0-8160-6824-1

Set ISBN: 978-0-8160-7218-7

Chelsea House books are available at special discounts when purchased in bulk quantities for businesses, associations, institutions, or sales promotions. Please call our Special Sales Department in New York at (212) 967-8800 or (800) 322-8755.

You can find Chelsea House on the World Wide Web at:
http://www.chelseahouse.com

The Brown Reference Group
(incorporating Andromeda Oxford Limited)
8 Chapel Place, Rivington Street
London EC2A 3DQ
www.brownreference.com

For The Brown Reference Group plc:
Editorial Director: Lindsey Lowe
Project Editor: Graham Bateman
Editor: Virginia Carter
Design: Steve McCurdy
Senior Managing Editor: Tim Cooke

Printed in Singapore

10 9 8 7 6 5 4 3 2 1

Contents

Introduction

THIS BOOK IS ABOUT MESOPOTAMIA—THE LAND BETWEEN THE Tigris and Euphrates Rivers—and the ancient Near East. It covers the present-day country of Iraq as well as parts of Iran, Turkey, Syria, Lebanon, and Israel. The region is varied in geography and climate, ranging from deserts to forested mountains and fertile river plains.

More than 12,000 years ago people of this region were among the first to change from a hunting-and-gathering, wandering lifestyle to settled farming communities. Many of the plants and animals on which modern European agriculture is based were first domesticated (brought under human control) in the Near East.

The first cities in the world also emerged in Mesopotamia, by about 4000 B.C.E., and influenced the surrounding cultures. The ancient Greeks and Romans learned from Mesopotamian civilization, and passed on their cultural heritage to Europe. For this reason Mesopotamia has been called the "cradle of civilization."

In recent times the Near East, unique in its contribution to human history, has been the scene of much conflict: first the Iran–Iraq War, and then the two Gulf Wars, of 1991 and 2003. Many wars have been fought in Mesopotamia from earliest times. The first kings, dating from about 3000 B.C.E., were originally leaders chosen by the people to defend city-states in times of war. By 2300 B.C.E. kings had become permanent heads of state, attending not only to military matters but also to the welfare of the population.

Rulers were thought to be responsible to the gods, even though some of them, such as the Assyrian, Babylonian, and Persian kings, ruled vast empires. The empire of Darius III was conquered by Alexander the Great in 331 B.C.E. From then on, the civilization of the ancient Near East went into decline, to be replaced by the newly powerful Hellenistic (Greek-speaking) culture.

Ancient Mesopotamia is divided into two parts. Part One, **The Land and the People**, traces the development of hunter-gatherer societies through village life to urban (city) life. It describes the domestication of plants and animals, and technological inventions such as clay bricks and pottery and the first writing. Part Two, **Kingdoms and Empires**, charts the rise and fall of the great kingdoms and empires of the Near East. These began with the reign of the Semitic king Sargon of Agade (2334–2279 B.C.E.) and ended with the Persian dynasty.

Most of the evidence for the history of Mesopotamia and the surrounding cultures comes from archaeological excavations. Special features in the book focus on the contribution of outstanding sites and the impact of war and looting on the archaeological heritage of Iraq.

Maps are an important part of the book. In Part One they show where technological changes began and spread in the Near East. In Part Two they show how empires grew and then faded, to be replaced by others. Location maps accompany each special spread, so that the sites may be easily identified.

Many of the pages list the names and dates of the cultures and kings of the period. Kings are usually grouped according to the dynasty (ruling family or line) to which they belonged. The spelling of names is often uncertain, and other versions can be found. Sargon, for example, may also be written as Sharruken. In *Ancient Mesopotamia* the easiest and most popular form of these names has usually been used. Similarly, many of the dates are not definite and should only be used as an approximate guide.

The Glossary on page 92 explains archaeological and technical terms and also defines the names of periods and dynasties. The Gazetteer on page 93 lists sites in alphabetical order, giving their latitude and longitude, as well as their modern locations.

The section entitled Further Reading provides a list of books and Web sites that we hope will interest you after reading *Ancient Mesopotamia*.

Abbreviations used in this book
B.C.E. = Before Common Era (also called B.C.). C.E. = Common Era (also called A.D.). c. = *circa* (about). ch. = chapter. chs = chapters.
mi = miles; ft = feet; in = inches.
km = kilometers; m = meters; cm = centimeters.

▶ Cuneiform (wedge-shaped) writing carved over the relief sculpture from a ninth-century B.C.E. palace at Kalhu.

Timelines

	12,000 B.C.E.	10,000 B.C.E.	7000 B.C.E.	4000 B.C.E.	3000 B.C.E.
ARCHAEOLOGICAL Period	EPI-PALEOLITHIC (MESOLITHIC)	PROTO-NEOLITHIC	ACERAMIC NEOLITHIC	NEOLITHIC	SUMERIAN	EARLY BRONZE AGE

TECHNICAL INVENTIONS

Hunting and gathering
Dog domesticated
Microlithic flint tools

Villages
Basketry
Grain roasting
Sheep herded
Farming—grain crops
Mud-bricks
Weaving
Pottery
Early copper tools

Ox plow
Cattle domesticated
Potter's wheel
Baked mud-bricks
Pottery kilns
Irrigation
Boats

Cities
Donkeys domesticated
Carts
Copper weapons
Cylinder seals
Cuneiform writing

City-states
Lost-wax method of casting metal
Gold- and silversmithin

Stone bird head from Nemrik, c.7500 B.C.E.

Flint arrowheads from Tell Brak.

Susa A bowl, c.4000 B.C.E.

Metal daggers from the Royal Cemetery of Ur, c.2600 B.C.E.

ART AND ARCHITECTURE

Round huts

Plastered skulls

Stone sculptures
Rectangular houses

Clay figurines

Tripartite temples

Walled cities

Cone mosaics
"Uruk Mona Lisa"
"Warka vase"
Palaces

Major Events
MESOPOTAMIA

End of Ice Age

✴ Shanidar Cave

✴ Zawi Chemi Shanidar

Hassuna, Samarra, Halaf, Ubaid

Uruk

✴ Tell Madhhur

✴ Ur

Jamdat Nasr
✴ Mari
Early Dynastic
Nippur
✴ Uruk

LEVANT

✴ Mt Carmel

✴ Jericho

Halaf

Ubaid

IRAN

✴ Choga Mami

Bronze and silver stag from Alaca Huyuk, c.2300 B.C.E.

ANATOLIA

✴ Chatal Hüyuk

EGYPT

Printed stone mask from Nahal Hemar, c.10,000 B.C.E.

Pre-Dynastic

✴ denotes important site of the period   ▲ denotes a king   words underlined are historical periods

2500 B.C.E.	2000 B.C.E.	1500 B.C.E.	1000 B.C.E.	750 B.C.E.	600 B.C.E.	300 B.C.E.
AKKADIAN	MIDDLE BRONZE AGE	LATE BRONZE AGE	IRON AGE			

Armies

Horse domesticated
Law codes
Sumerian King List
Hammurabi's law code

Glazed pottery
Glass
Chariots

Cavalry
Alphabet—Aramaic writing

Battering-ram
Siege engine

*Choga Zanbil ziggurat,
c.1200 B.C.E.*

*Faience mask from
Tell al-Rimah, c.1350 B.C.E.*

*Samarian ivory,
c.900 B.C.E.*

*Horse head on a relief from
Dur-Sharrukin, c.710 B.C.E.*

Ziggurats

Glazed, molded bricks

Ivory carving

Kudurru stones

Royal library, Nineveh

Hanging Gardens, Babylon

Kings of Agade
▲ Sargon
▲ Naram-Sin

Third Dynasty of Ur
Isin–Larsa

Old Babylonian

Assyrian
▲ Shamshi-Adad
(Amorites)
Mittani
Kassites

Middle Babylonian

✳ Ashur
(Aramaeans)

Late Babylonian

Middle Assyrian

✳ Nineveh

Medes

✳ Kalhu
Late Assyrian
▲ Tiglath-Pileser
▲ Sargon
▲ Sennacherib
▲ Esarhaddon
▲ Ashurbanipal
✳ Babylon
New Babylonians

Persians
▲ Nabopolassar
▲ Nebuchadrezzar

▲ Alexander

✳ Ebla

Mittani

(Sea Peoples)
(Philistines)
(Israelites)

Israel and Judah
David
Solomon

Assyrian victory

Exile of Jews to Babylon

*Head of blue paste from
Persepolis, c.450 B.C.E.*

*Bronze weight from
Kalhu, c.700 B.C.E.*

Persians—Cyrus, Darius
✳ Susa

(Hurrians)

Hittites

Lydians
Croesus

New Kingdom

Amarna Letters

Ramesses III

(Sea Peoples)

Cambyses

Part One

The Land and the People

▲ An Akkadian relief from about 2300 B.C.E. showing naked prisoners of war.

▶ Stairs leading to the top of the ziggurat at Ur, where a temple once stood.

Physical Background

THE LANDS WHERE THE FIRST CIVILIZATIONS developed stretched from the Gulf (often known as either the Arabian or the Persian Gulf) through modern Iraq to Syria and the Levant (present-day Lebanon and Israel) on the Mediterranean coast. This area of West Asia is often called the Fertile Crescent.

The heartland of this cradle of human history was Mesopotamia—the flat plain of rich soil that was watered by the Tigris and Euphrates rivers. These two rivers rise in the mountainous region of northeastern Turkey and drain into the Gulf.

The Zagros Mountains in modern Iran formed the eastern barrier to this region. In the west and south were the desolate lands of the Syrian and Arabian deserts.

Climate and environment

When the last Ice Age ended, in about 12,000 B.C.E., the climate of West Asia became similar to what it is today. The vegetation (plant life) changed because of the warmer temperatures.

The mountains of Iran, Turkey, and the Mediterranean coast became forested with oak, cedar, and pine trees. These woods and forests became the home of deer, wild sheep and goats, wolves, and leopards. Wild wheat and barley also grew here.

The northern part of Mesopotamia consisted of rolling grasslands where boars, oxen, and even lions roamed. The southern part of Mesopotamia, toward the Gulf, hosted a wealth of bird life that lived in its many swamps and marshes.

Water

People could only live permanently in the areas where there were constant supplies of water. Rainfall was scarce in Mesopotamia, but the Tigris and Euphrates were mighty rivers, fed by the melting snows of the Zagros and Taurus mountains. With their many lesser tributary rivers, they provided a lifeline throughout Mesopotamia. Irrigation canals were cut from the rivers and their tributaries to bring the water directly to the fields.

◄ An oasis in the desert. Oases—areas that are fertile because water is present— are quite common in deserts. Often the water comes from an underground spring. Palm trees occur naturally at oases and, with irrigation, crops can be grown, allowing orchards and gardens to thrive.

Scale 1 : 14 280 000
0   400km
0   300 m

Irrigation

Unlike the Nile River, which flooded Egypt with such regularity that it could be calculated, the Tigris and Euphrates rivers were unpredictable and unreliable. They could rise in flood, becoming raging muddy torrents, or they could change their courses overnight and in doing so destroy the villages that lined their banks.

In time, the people of the river plains learned to build irrigation systems (consisting of canals and ditches) that helped them control the flow of water and channel it to their food crops. After that the "land between the rivers" (which is what the Greek name Mesopotamia means) became highly productive for farming.

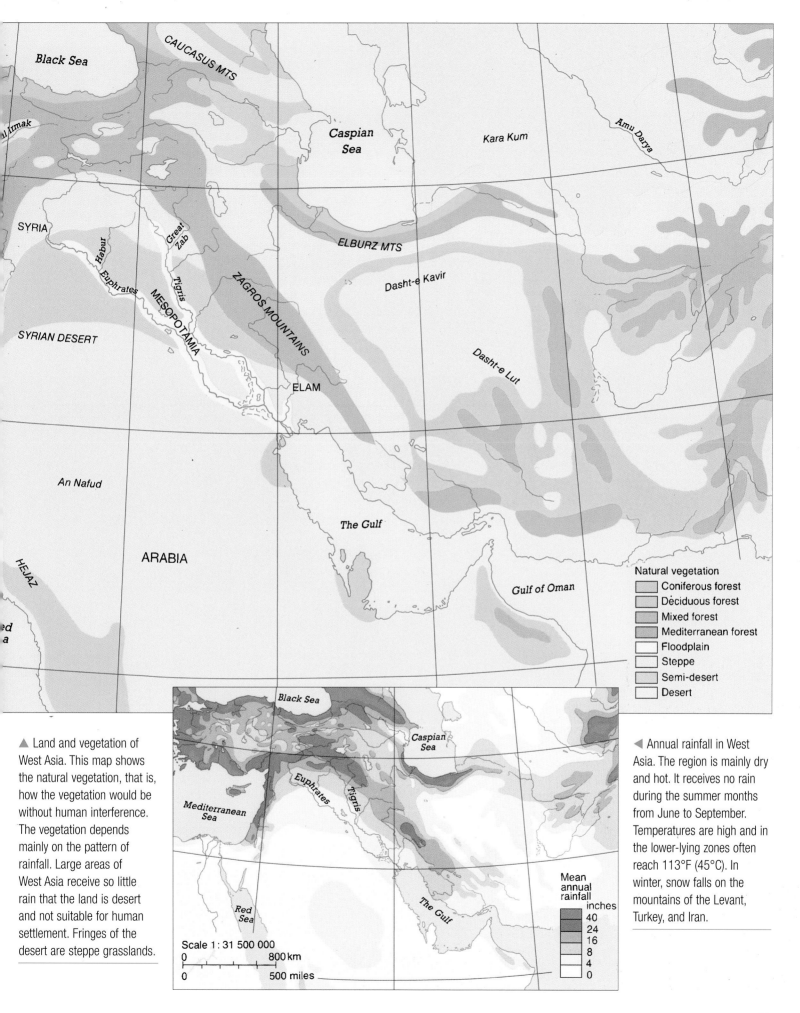

Black Sea

CAUCASUS MTS

Caspian
Sea

Kara Kum

Amu Darya

ll Irmak

SYRIA

Habur

Great
Zab

Euphrates

Tigris

MESOPOTAMIA

ELBURZ MTS

ZAGROS MOUNTAINS

Dasht-e Kavir

SYRIAN DESERT

Dasht-e Lut

ELAM

An Nafud

The Gulf

ARABIA

Gulf of Oman

HEJAZ

ed
a

Natural vegetation

Coniferous forest
Deciduous forest
Mixed forest
Mediterranean forest
Floodplain
Steppe
Semi-desert
Desert

Black Sea

Caspian
Sea

Euphrates

Tigris

Mediterranean
Sea

Red
Sea

The Gulf

**Mean
annual
rainfall**
inches
40
24
16
8
4
0

Scale 1 : 31 500 000
0   800 km
0   500 miles

▲ Land and vegetation of
West Asia. This map shows
the natural vegetation, that is,
how the vegetation would be
without human interference.
The vegetation depends
mainly on the pattern of
rainfall. Large areas of
West Asia receive so little
rain that the land is desert
and not suitable for human
settlement. Fringes of the
desert are steppe grasslands.

◄ Annual rainfall in West
Asia. The region is mainly dry
and hot. It receives no rain
during the summer months
from June to September.
Temperatures are high and in
the lower-lying zones often
reach 113°F (45°C). In
winter, snow falls on the
mountains of the Levant,
Turkey, and Iran.

11

Archaeology in West Asia

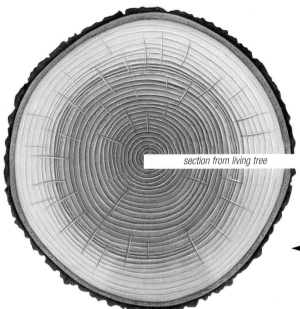

section from living tree

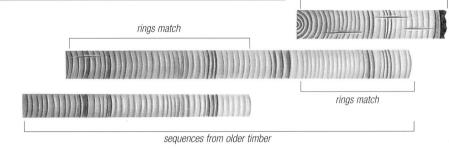

▼ The trunk of a tree shows rings when it is sawn in half. Each ring equals a year's growth: the warmer the conditions in any year, the wider the ring will be. By adding up the number of rings, the age of the tree can be worked out, even if it is thousands of years old. Sequences of rings where the years of growth are known can be matched with the ring patterns of an ancient piece of timber, telling us its age.

sequence from living tree

rings match

rings match

sequences from older timber

time back in past

ARCHAEOLOGY IS THE SCIENTIFIC STUDY OF the human past using the physical traces left by early people. This has told us a lot about the history of West Asia. In the nineteenth century, archaeologists from Europe and America dug up sites to find objects for their museums. Today, archaeology tries to reconstruct from its findings how society was organized.

Excavating a site

Archaeologists do a variety of jobs, from supervising the people who physically dig the site to recording every detail about the different levels that are exposed. The oldest remains are usually at the lowest levels, with the most recent closest to the surface.

Archaeological "finds" may range from gold coins and beautiful jewelry to hundreds or thousands of pieces of broken pottery (sherds), fragments of animal bones, and tools made of stone (flint). Even the seeds of plants are collected, by passing the soil in which they are found through sieves. Seeds give information about crops and foods. Important finds that are broken are repaired, and there are special treatments for ivory, wood, metal items, and inscriptions (carved or engraved words).

The contours (outline) of excavated sites used to be mapped painstakingly by hand, but nowadays they are often charted using a computer. More and more advanced scientific techniques are being used in archaeology today, including new discoveries by satellite photography (using infrared film) and global positioning systems.

▶ A worker uses a paintbrush to dust away the soil from pieces of pottery. The woman is placing them into the rubber basket. The pottery is taken away and washed carefully so that any decoration or inscriptions will not be removed. The location of each sherd is noted to help build a profile of the site's occupation.

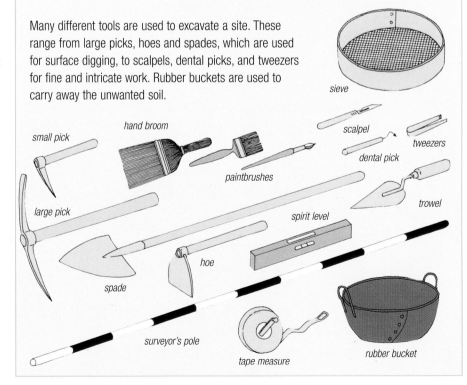

Many different tools are used to excavate a site. These range from large picks, hoes and spades, which are used for surface digging, to scalpels, dental picks, and tweezers for fine and intricate work. Rubber buckets are used to carry away the unwanted soil.

sieve

small pick

hand broom

scalpel

tweezers

dental pick

paintbrushes

large pick

trowel

spirit level

hoe

spade

surveyor's pole

tape measure

rubber bucket

◀ Archaeologists at work. The team has unearthed the stone wall topped by layers of mud-brick. After they have drawn it, they will demolish it to find out what is beneath. A worker climbs the ladder with a bucket of soil, which is dumped on to the nearby piles. The dagger, skeleton, broken pots, and other items will be uncovered as the lower levels are excavated.

▼ Fragile objects have to be very carefully treated. These statuettes were made from mud plastered on a reed framework. The process of sticking together all the fragments is a painstaking and expensive job that takes many months.

Building up a picture from the site

The layout of the buildings in the different layers of the excavation shows archaeologists how the site developed. Major features, such as city walls and gates, may show similarities with other sites and can therefore help establish the site's dating sequence or chronology.

The chronology also can be worked out from the pottery found, because certain shapes were used in different periods. Coins are very useful for working out the date of a site, but coins are not found in periods earlier than the seventh century B.C.E. Inscriptions may also supply historical information.

Radio carbon dating, a sophisticated scientific technique, can show the age of wooden objects. However, the results may not be of great value for dating a site, because the objects may originally have come from elsewhere. They may therefore show trade links between the excavated site and other areas of West Asia. Pottery excavated from the site may supply similar evidence. Pottery can be dated by thermoluminescence, which measures the decay of radioactive elements in the clay.

Early Peoples (to 11,000 B.C.E.)

IN THE PALEOLITHIC, OR OLD STONE AGE, *Homo sapiens*, or modern humans, lived alongside Neanderthal humans (*Homo neanderthalensis*). Both groups lived as hunter-gatherers. They obtained their food by hunting wild animals and collecting plants and other edible items. They took shelter in caves, such as Mount Carmel (now in Israel) and Shanidar (now in Iraq).

After the last great Ice Age ended, *Homo sapiens* began to grow crops (such as barley and wheat) and to herd animals (such as sheep and goats) in West Asia in about 11,000–9000 B.C.E. This change in food production happened over the course of thousands of years, and people gradually began to settle in permanent villages.

Near East Paleolithic and Mesolithic cultures

Cultures are represented by named archaeological sites and by layers in the ground where the appropriate objects were found.

Lower Paleolithic 85,000–60,000 B.C.E. ACHEULEAN culture
Site: Shanidar Cave (Base), Iraq

Middle Paleolithic 60,000–35,000 B.C.E. MOUSTERIAN culture
Site: Shanidar Cave (Layers D, C), Iraq
40,000 B.C.E. *Homo sapiens* appears

Upper Paleolithic 35,000–18,000 B.C.E. BARADOSTIAN cultures
Sites: Kebara (Layer D), Israel; Zarzi, Iraq

Epi-Paleolithic (Mesolithic) 18,000–12,000 B.C.E. ZARZIAN culture
End of the last Ice Age
Sites: Kebara (Layers C, B), Israel; M'Lefaat, Iraq; Karim Shahir, Iraq; Shanidar Cave (Layer B), Iraq; Zawi Chemi Shanidar (B), Iraq; Mt Carmel, Israel

▼ Early agriculture. Barley and wheat were first cultivated in the foothills of northern Mesopotamia between about 11,000 B.C.E. and 9000 B.C.E. By about 5000 B.C.E. these crops were grown in the Caucasus to the north, in Egypt to the south, to the west in Anatolia (Turkey) and southeastern Europe, and eastward in Iran and even India. In China and southeast Asia, rice and millet were being cultivated.

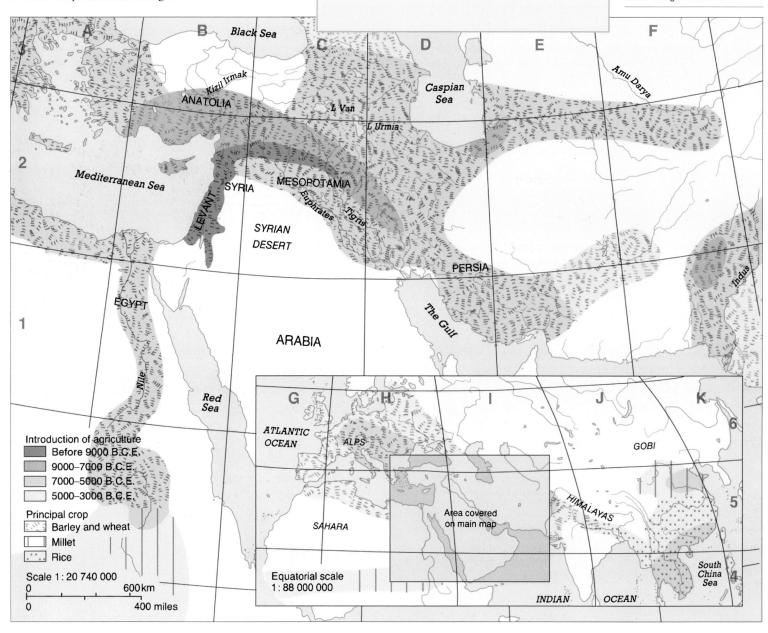

Introduction of agriculture
- Before 9000 B.C.E.
- 9000–7000 B.C.E.
- 7000–5000 B.C.E.
- 5000–3000 B.C.E.

Principal crop
- Barley and wheat
- Millet
- Rice

Scale 1 : 20 740 000
0 — 600km
0 — 400 miles

Equatorial scale 1 : 88 000 000

Area covered on main map

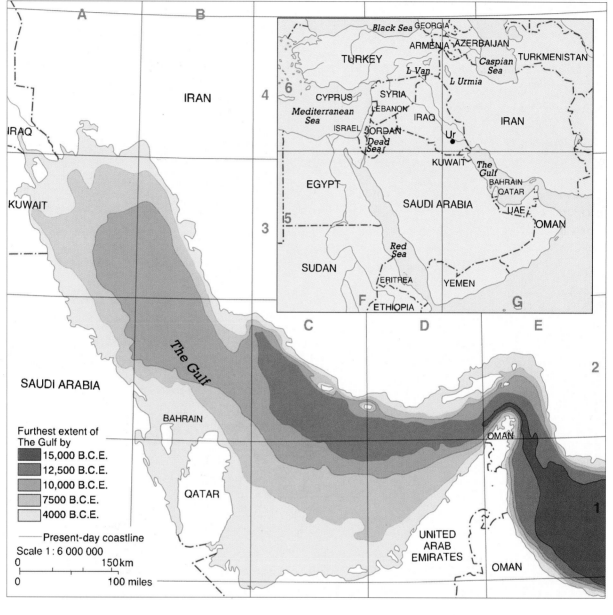

► The changing shape of the Gulf. The Gulf has been growing in size since 15,000 B.C.E., when sea levels were about 330 ft (100 m) lower than today. As the last Ice Age ended, sea levels rose with the warmer temperatures. Since 4000 B.C.E. sea levels have remained almost the same, but silting from the Tigris and Euphrates rivers has significantly changed the coastline. These maps show the boundaries of present-day countries.

Furthest extent of The Gulf by
- 15,000 B.C.E.
- 12,500 B.C.E.
- 10,000 B.C.E.
- 7500 B.C.E.
- 4000 B.C.E.

— Present-day coastline

Scale 1 : 6 000 000

0 — 150km

0 — 100 miles

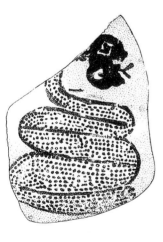

▲ A snake painted on a piece of pottery dating from before 5000 B.C.E. Many such pottery decorations show the wild animals and birds that lived in ancient West Asia.

The Neolithic revolution

The change from hunter-gatherer societies transformed the human lifestyle and is known as the "Neolithic revolution" (Neolithic means New Stone Age). The first settlements were in Palestine and the upper Euphrates valley of Syria. They seem to have developed separately rather than coming from a single center.

Climatic changes that took place in West Asia after the last Ice Age from about 12,000 B.C.E. resulted in higher temperatures, different forms of vegetation, and, perhaps, fewer animals. The warmer temperatures resulted in an increase in the human population. The combination of these events may have helped trigger the Neolithic revolution.

Stone technology

To cater to the new methods of food production new tools had to be developed. Most were made from flint or other stone, using such techniques as chipping, flaking, "pecking," and grinding. Some were fixed to bone or antler handles.

Toward the end of the Paleolithic period, very small flints began to appear. Called microliths, they come in a number of different shapes. Some set in bone sickle handles (curved cutting tools) have been found at Mount Carmel.

Microlith flints were sharper and more efficient than the larger tools of the Paleolithic or Old Stone Age. They show that people collected grains, but they do not prove that they already cultivated plants.

Mesopotamian Sites

Shanidar

SHANIDAR CAVE IS LOCATED NEAR THE Great Zab River in the rugged Zagros Mountains of Iraqi Kurdistan. As early as 100,000 B.C.E. small groups of Neanderthal people sheltered here during the cold winter months. They hunted wild sheep, pigs, cattle, and goats.

Several of the cave-dwellers appear to have been killed by rockfalls. Pollen deposits found with skeletons show that Neanderthal people may have also buried their dead, sometimes with flowers. Their stone tools belong to the Middle Paleolithic Mousterian culture.

Modern humans (*Homo sapiens*) appeared at Shanidar in about 40,000 B.C.E. Their tools were more advanced than those of the Neanderthals, who died out by 33,000 B.C.E. There are no signs of people living at Shanidar between 28,000 B.C.E. and 12,000 B.C.E. Later tools from the Epi-Paleolithic culture found there are made of obsidian (a dark, glassy, volcanic rock), indicating trade with southeast Turkey. Twenty-six skeletons, some with grave goods, were buried in the cave in about 10,000 B.C.E. One of the skeletons, that of a man, had had his arm amputated, perhaps because of a disease or injury.

▼ Life at Zawi Chemi Shanidar. Hunters are gathered around the fire. One is making a flint spearhead by flaking it into a sharp point. Another man has been collecting firewood from the nearby oak forests. The men wear garments made from animal skins. Skins were also used to make the roofs of the round huts.

Zawi Chemi Shanidar

Zawi Chemi Shanidar, 1.8 miles (3 km) from Shanidar Cave, bridges the period between the Epi-Paleolithic and the first fully developed villages, such as Jarmo. The stone tools used were similar to earlier ones, but new types also emerged. As at Shanidar Cave, there was some trading in types of stone used for toolmaking.

At three different periods, round huts of about 13 feet (4 m) in diameter were built using river boulders. People may have lived at Zawi Chemi Shanidar through the summer and returned to

▼ Women at Zawi Chemi Shanidar scrape and stretch the skin of a red deer. They may have also made the fiber baskets outside the hut doorways, used for collecting such food as snails. Goats or sheep are kept behind the wicker fence.

Shanidar Cave for the winter. Pollen samples found there suggest that wild wheat and barley grew nearby, but there were also attempts at cultivation. The people of Zawi Chemi Shanidar lived from hunting wild animals, but large numbers of bones from young animals indicate that they also practiced herding sheep and goats.

A pile of eagles' wing bones and 15 goats' skulls were also found at the site. This suggests that people practiced religious ceremonies there. Zawi Chemi Shanidar was settled at the same time as many sites in the Levant, but there are no direct links.

Early Village Life

BY 10,000 B.C.E. PEOPLE BEGAN TO SETTLE in villages. Many of these villages were very small, covering less than 2.5 acres (1 ha)—about the area of a small field. Round huts were built sunk partly into the ground for insulation against extremes of heat and cold.

The earliest group of round huts dates from as long ago as 15,000 B.C.E. at Ain Gev on the banks of the Sea of Galilee. Much later, houses became rectangular with plastered walls, and they sometimes had several rooms. Both stages of housing were found among the 26 levels of occupation at Beidha in present-day southern Jordan.

Tools, materials, and crafts

People still made many tools from stone. Some had chisel edges and may have been used to cut wood, which was then fashioned into other tools. Wooden implements may have been used in harvesting or for animal traps. Unlike stone, wood decays, but at Nahal Hemar in modern Israel a wooden-handled sickle has been found.

Bone and horn from slaughtered animals made a variety of tools that were used for fishing and the preparation of hides (animal skins), as well as for basketry, weaving, and rope-making. Evidence of matting dating from as early as 10,000 B.C.E. has been found at Shanidar Cave. Tools used by Native Americans in North America today show how these crafts were practiced.

Nahal Hemar

Some very useful finds have been made at Nahal Hemar, a cave in the Judaean desert near the Dead Sea. Until this discovery was made in 1938, the only evidence of reed matting and basketry was a few impressions left in clay.

Although archaeologists found that the people did not use or make clay pots, they did discover in the cave fragments of textiles, wood, arrowheads, flint utensils, nets, and basketry dating from about 7000 B.C.E. They had been preserved by the extremely dry climate. Hundreds of pieces of cord, ranging from fine string to thick rope, show the high technical skills of the people at this site. Baskets made from coils of twisted cord and coated in bitumen (a naturally occurring tar) may have been used to carry and store water.

Among the ritual or religious objects unearthed at Nahal Hemar were a stone mask with a human head, heads made of wood and clay, four small carved bone human heads, and several adult skulls. These items may have been part of a cult of ancestor-worship, which was common among early peoples.

▼ This round house at Qermez Dere in northern Iraq was built partly sunk into the ground. Sunken houses were easier to build and also had better insulation against the climate. The roof, possibly made of skins, may have been held up by wooden poles. The stone walls were covered with mud. Cooking was done on the hearth. The stone-and-plaster pillar and the skulls indicate that ritual cults had developed.

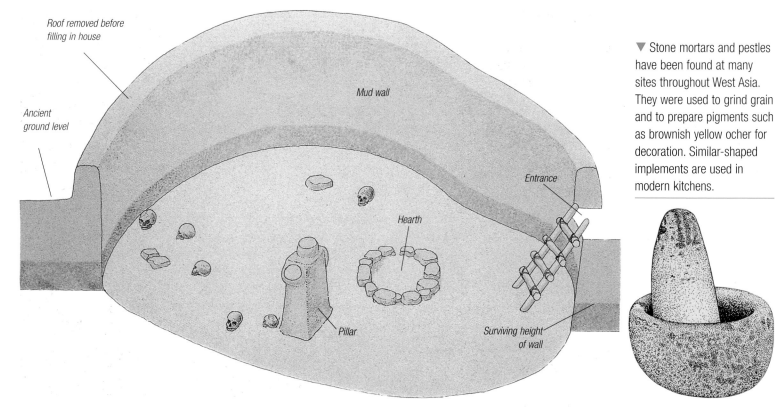

Roof removed before filling in house

Ancient ground level

Mud wall

Hearth

Entrance

Pillar

Surviving height of wall

▼ Stone mortars and pestles have been found at many sites throughout West Asia. They were used to grind grain and to prepare pigments such as brownish yellow ocher for decoration. Similar-shaped implements are used in modern kitchens.

◄ Modern houses in villages in West Asia are still built of mud-brick. Their flat roofs, made of matting laid upon timber beams, can be used for living space, sleeping, and storage.

◄ Male and female statuettes from a large collection found at Ain Ghazal, near Amman in Jordan. They are made of reed plastered with clay. The exact purpose of these figures is unknown, but must have been linked to rituals or religious practice.

Widespread ritual cults

Plastered and decorated skulls, sometimes with shells in their eye sockets, have been found at many sites from the same period in the Levant, including Jericho, Am Mallaha, Mount Carmel, and Ain Chazal. The skulls were buried under the floors of houses. At Nemrik, in northern Mesopotamia, 15 stylized stone sculptures of birds, animals, and humans were discovered. These may have been totems (symbolic objects used in rituals).

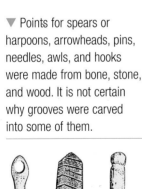

▼ Points for spears or harpoons, arrowheads, pins, needles, awls, and hooks were made from bone, stone, and wood. It is not certain why grooves were carved into some of them.

▼ Sickles were used to cut grasses and reeds. They were often made from bone. The tiny microlith flint blades were fixed to the handle of the tool with bitumen.

▶ Textiles were woven from plant fibers, probably flax (linen), in several ways. Pairs of weft threads were twisted around the warps to produce a dense weave called close twining (top). With spaced twining, the twisted threads were separated (center). Normal, or tabby, weaving (below) was also carried out. Weaving was done by hand, using tools made from the long bones of animals. Shuttles that were pointed at one end and pierced with a hole at the other have been found at Ghassul in Jordan.

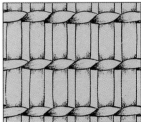

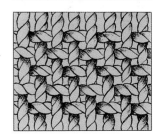

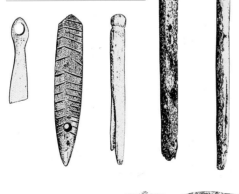

First Farmers (11,000–9300 B.C.E.)

W EST ASIA WAS ONE OF THE FIRST regions in the world where agriculture developed about 13,000 years ago. Wild ancestors of the grains that were cultivated and of the animals that were domesticated first appeared in the Levant and on the hills flanking the north Mesopotamian and Syrian plains.

Grain collection

The Neolithic revolution in the Levant began about 11,000 B.C.E. with the Natufian period. Sickles and grinding stones from this period found at Mount Carmel on the shores of the Mediterranean indicate that cereals were an important part of the diet.

At Ain Mallaha in Syria a number of bell-shaped storage pits were discovered. These were lined with plaster and used to store grain. At Mureybet in northern Syria there were pits for roasting grain. It is not known whether these cereals were cultivated or whether they were only gathered.

◀ The first farmers probably winnowed their grain (to separate edible grain from outer chaff) like this present-day Arab farmer. His fork may be based on an ancient design. Few early wooden tools have survived.

▼ Settlements and farmers. After the last Ice Age, people began to establish villages in areas of good rainfall (more than 8 in/20 cm a year) where cereals grew naturally and animals were plentiful. Such early village sites span the Fertile Crescent from the Levant through northern Syria to Kurdistan and Iraq.

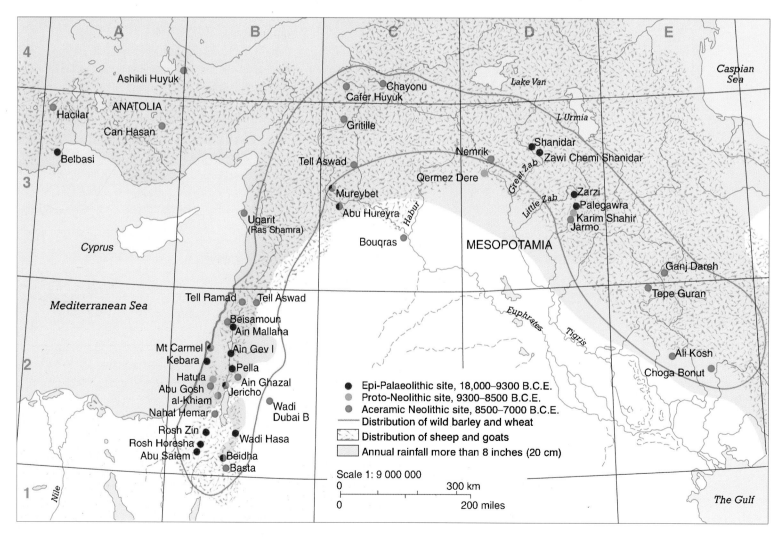

- ● Epi-Palaeolithic site, 18,000–9300 B.C.E.
- ● Proto-Neolithic site, 9300–8500 B.C.E.
- ● Aceramic Neolithic site, 8500–7000 B.C.E.
- ── Distribution of wild barley and wheat
- ▨ Distribution of sheep and goats
- ▫ Annual rainfall more than 8 inches (20 cm)

Scale 1: 9 000 000
0 — 300 km
0 — 200 miles

▶ The Taurus Mountains dominate this valley in Cilicia, southern Turkey. It lies in the rainfall zone where crops were grown in fields without irrigation. Herds grazed in the pastures during the winter months and in the summer were taken up the mountains to feed.

▼ Stages in the domestication of wheat in West Asia. Emmer wheat was a natural hybrid (cross-bred offspring) of einkorn wheat and goat grass. Further selective breeding helped produce wheat plants ideal for harvesting and threshing.

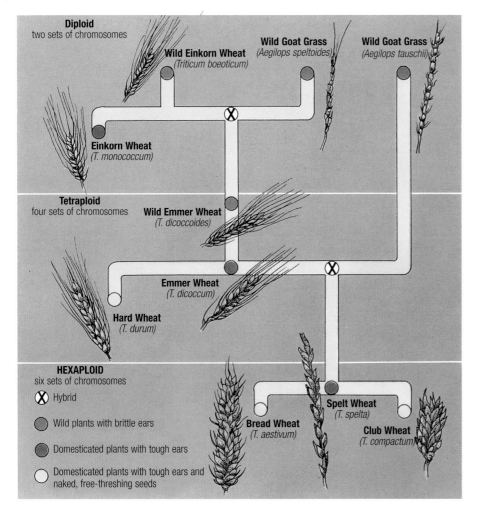

Grain cultivation

The Natufian diet included wild barley and two kinds of wheat that grew naturally in West Asia. Einkorn wheat and emmer wheat provided the seed for the first crops. In these first attempts at genetic engineering, domestic varieties of wheat were developed over generations of selective planting and harvesting. Other cereals, such as barley, were also bred to create strains that yielded more seed. This selection process helped people produce more food. By 8000 B.C.E. most communities in West Asia grew cereals.

Animal husbandry

People gradually became less reliant on hunting for food and began to develop herding, then farming, techniques. We do not know exactly how this happened—the process of domestication took several thousand years and was complicated. Many animals that were native to West Asia were eventually domesticated. For example, wolves were domesticated to become dogs, "mouflons" became sheep, and aurochs (wild cattle) became cows.

Natufian sites including Mount Carmel and Abu Hureyra in Syria show that wild animals (gazelle, boar, deer) were commonly eaten. Large numbers of bones from young animals suggest that herding and selective culling (choosing which animals would remain in the herd) took place.

21

Animals in Daily Life

OGS SEEM TO HAVE BEEN THE FIRST animals to be tamed. A dog's jawbone from 11,000 B.C.E. has been found at Palegawra in northeastern Iraq. At Ain Mallaha a skeleton of a young puppy dated to 10,000 B.C.E. was buried in a grave with a woman. Dogs were domesticated from wolves and were probably used to help people hunt wild animals for food.

Sheep and goats

Not all wild animals could be domesticated. Large amounts of bones left at Natufian sites in the Levant show that gazelles were a major part of the diet. At Abu Hureyra villagers were hunting gazelles and harvesting wild cereals around 9500 B.C.E. Attempts to herd gazelles seem to have failed, and instead sheep—which were not native to the region—were introduced from northern zones.

Sheep and goats formed an important part of the farming economy. They provided people with meat, hides, milk, and fleece. The first domestic sheep appeared in about 11,000 B.C.E. at Zawi Chemi Shanidar. Goats were domesticated at Tepe Asiab, in the Zagros Mountains.

These animals also had a ritual, or religious, importance. Goats' skulls were found at Zawi Chemi Shanidar, along with wing bones of large birds. Two rams' skulls were found attached, one above the other, to the walls of a shrine at Ganj Dareh.

▲ A procession of goats, sheep, and cattle, inlaid in bone on the "Standard of Ur" (probably the sounding box of a musical instrument). The men's clothes shown here were made from the fine wool of domesticated sheep, which was much softer than the rough hairy fleece of wild sheep.

▼ Arab warriors on camels fleeing from the Assyrian army. Camels were introduced into Mesopotamia from Arabia between 2000 B.C.E. and 1000 B.C.E. They were used for transportation and war.

Origin of common farm animals

Domesticated animal	Wild ancestor	Region	Date
Dog	Wolf	West Asia	c.11,000 B.C.E.
Goat	Bezoar goat	West Asia	c.8500 B.C.E.
Sheep	Asiatic mouflon	West Asia	c.8000 B.C.E.
Pig	Wild boar	West Asia	c.7500 B.C.E.
Cattle	Auroch	West Asia	c.7000 B.C.E.
Cat	Wild cat	West Asia	c.7000 B.C.E.
Chicken	Red jungle fowl	China	c.6000 B.C.E.
Llama	Guanaco	Andes	c.5000 B.C.E.
Donkey	Wild ass	West Asia	c.4000 B.C.E.
Horse	Tarpan	Southern Russia	c.4000 B.C.E.
Camel	Wild camel	?Southern Arabia/?Southern Central Asia	c.3000 B.C.E.
Guinea pig	Cavy	Peru	c.2000 B.C.E.
Rabbit	Wild rabbit	Spain	c.1000 B.C.E.
Turkey	Wild turkey	Mexico	c.300 B.C.E.

Cattle

Wild cattle (aurochs) roamed West Asia and were hunted for their meat and hides. At Chatal Hüyuk in central Turkey, cattle were domesticated by 6000 B.C.E. They were an important source of food and their skeletons make up 90 percent of the animal bones found at this site.

Bulls' skulls have been found in several shrines. In one, they were situated near a painting of vultures attacking headless corpses. At Mureybit on the Euphrates River in northern Syria, fragments of an ox's skull were deliberately buried in a clay bench. In Anatolia the bull became associated with the weather or storm god.

▶ A fine relief of a mastiff being taken out hunting. Hunting dogs were bred for size and strength. Dog skeletons found in graves at Eridu, Iraq, and dating from about 5000 B.C.E. have been identified as greyhounds. They are the ancestors of the saluki, which is still prized today in Arabia for its hunting skills.

◀ A ninth-century B.C.E. carving showing horses being groomed and fed. The onager, or wild ass, was native to West Asia. But the horse only arrived from the central Russian steppes in about 4000 B.C.E. Horses were used at first to pull chariots. In Sumerian times (about 2500 B.C.E.) they were thought to be inferior beasts which no gentleman would ride. A king or a noble would ride in a chariot pulled by asses. By 1000 B.C.E., however, cavalry formed very effective fighting units.

Technology and Trade

PEOPLE FIRST USED UNBAKED MUD-BRICK for building in about 8000 B.C.E. It was cheap, easy to make, and was more readily available than stone. The earliest bricks, from the Proto-Neolithic period (the earliest Neolithic), were made by hand and looked like a loaf of bread, with a flat base and a rounded top. Much later, houses became rectangular in shape when straight-sided mud-bricks were used.

Jericho

People lived at Jericho, in the Jordan valley, from 9000 B.C.E. Round huts built from cigar-shaped handmade bricks provide the earliest known use of mud-bricks. In about 8000 B.C.E. a huge, thick, stone wall was erected, surrounded by a large ditch. There was also a massive tower with a staircase inside. The wall and tower were probably built for defense and were recalled in the later biblical story of Joshua.

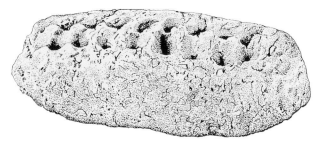

▶ An early mud-brick, shaped by the brickmaker's hand. He has pressed his thumbs into the top, leaving a herringbone pattern. This was not decoration, but done to fix the mortar and to let it "breathe."

▶ The city of Erbil in Kurdistan stands on a mound more than 165 feet (50 m) high. Mud-brick buildings decay and collapse in the climate of West Asia. New houses are built on the remains of the old ones. After many centuries the debris forms a mound, called a tell. On the flat Mesopotamian landscape, tells are very noticeable.

Using metals and clay

Major changes happened in about 8500 B.C.E. At Chayonu in Anatolia (modern Turkey), more than 100 copper beads, pins, and tools have been found. Copper may have come from a local source of ore rather than being smelted. Copper beads have also been discovered in the Zagros Mountains, at Ali Kosh. At the nearby site of Ganj Dareh, the rectangular buildings were made of long, handmade mud-bricks. Many human and animal figurines (small figures) modeled in clay and pottery vessels have also been found there.

At Mureybet, at the western end of the Fertile Crescent, four lightly fired clay pots were found in a house. This pottery can be dated to 8000 B.C.E. and is 500 years older than any other examples

▲ Later, mud-bricks became straight-sided, made from a mixture of mud, chopped straw, and water. The mixture is placed in a mold, before being left to dry in the sun for several days.

▶ Mud-bricks are still used in West Asia. Bricks can help date a building because their sizes and shapes vary in different periods. Square bricks were easier to use than other shapes.

previously found. A new industry had begun in West Asia. It signaled a major step in the history of technological development.

Trade

Jericho, an oasis town in the desert near the Dead Sea, was surrounded by a stone wall and a ditch. These defenses suggest that it was a trade center for salt and bitumen from the Dead Sea, cowrie shells from the Red Sea, turquoise and copper from the Sinai peninsula, and obsidian from Anatolia. Obsidian is a volcanic glass with a much sharper cutting edge than flint and was greatly sought after in the making of superior-quality tools. Copper was also used extensively for making tools.

All these products were widely traded throughout West Asia. Traders may have traveled distances of up to 500 miles (800 km). Because many items, such as textiles and skin products, have not survived, the full extent of the trade network cannot be known.

Clay-using cultures of West Asia

Periods are represented by named archaeological sites.

9000–8500 B.C.E. PROTO-NEOLITHIC PERIOD (PRE-POTTERY NEOLITHIC A)
Sites: Jericho, Jordan; Mureybet, Syria
First evidence of handmade bricks

8500–7000 B.C.E. ACERAMIC NEOLITHIC PERIOD (PRE-POTTERY NEOLITHIC B)
Sites: Jericho, Jordan; Ain Ghazal, Jordan; Beidha, Jordan; Mureybet, Syria; Tell Abu Hurerya, Syria; Chayonu, Turkey; Jarmo, Iraq; Ganj Dareh, Iran
Use of handmade bricks; rectangular houses with plaster floors; clay modeling of animal and human figurines

8000 B.C.E.
Site: Mureybet, Syria
First evidence of fired pottery

▲ Shells were sometimes inlaid in the eye sockets of skulls buried under the floors of houses at Jericho. The skull was separated from the skeleton after the rest of the body had decayed.

▲ A pot made from white ware, a type of lime plaster developed in about 8000 B.C.E. Before people used pottery, containers were made from many different materials.

▶ Raw materials and trade. The Zagros Mountains were rich in minerals and wood. Copper came from Sinai; obsidian and metals from Anatolia. Mesopotamia had bitumen deposits but lacked any other resources. Finding the source of a metal or stone helps us understand the development of trade.

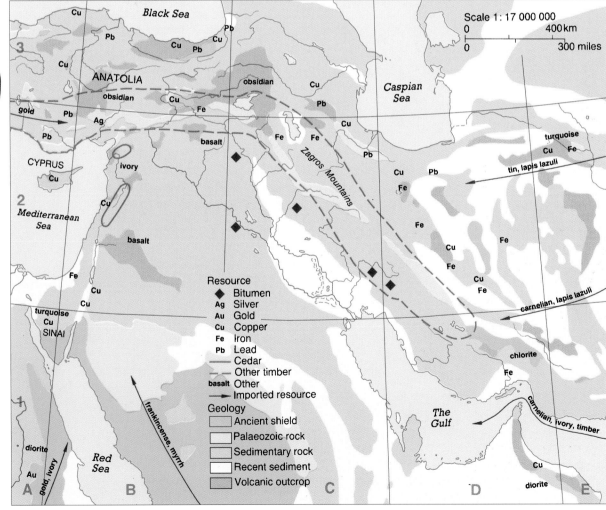

The Art of Pottery

AFTER 8000 B.C.E. PEOPLE WHO LIVED IN villages began using pottery throughout West Asia. Complete pottery vessels are sometimes found at archaeological sites, but usually only hundreds of sherds (pottery fragments) are discovered. Pottery was cheap, especially if it was locally produced. If a vessel broke, therefore, it was simply thrown away.

Baked clay, from which pottery is made, is almost indestructible and can survive all sorts of weather conditions. Even if a city was burned, the pottery fragments would survive. Many sites are covered with a layer of potsherds that are left after the wind and rain have washed away the surface soil. These remains provide archaeologists with a great deal of information about a site.

What pottery tells us about a site

Pottery can be used to date a site, especially those that date to times before the invention of writing. In different periods and at different places, pottery was produced in various ways and decorated with particular designs. From the range of sherds they collect at a site, archaeologists can work out when people lived there.

Similar pottery styles found at a number of sites in a region show that people lived in these places at about the same time. Different types of pottery tell us about changes in the settlement of a region over a period of hundreds or thousands of years. Where imported pottery (brought in by trade) is found, we can sometimes work out the links between different groups of people.

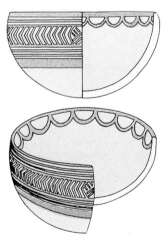

▼ Pottery vessels found in an excavation are drawn in cross-section so that archaeologists can compare the pottery types from different sites. The left-hand side shows the outside of the bowl and the right-hand side the inside. The drawing is made to scale and shows any decoration.

◄ This early, handmade pottery container from about 6500 B.C.E. is crudely made and only lightly fired. It is porous and could not be used to store liquids. The herringbone pattern on its surface was made using a sharp tool.

◀ Some pottery was decorated to a high artistic standard. The bowl on the left shows four ibexes (mountain goats) arranged in a cross pattern. It dates from about 5000 B.C.E., and the style is called Samarran. The multicolored plate on the right is from the Halaf period (6000–5400 B.C.E.). This fine pottery was only matched by the much later red-and-black Greek Attic ware.

How pottery was made

Pottery is made basically from clay, often mixed with an ingredient called a temper to reduce shrinkage or expansion. Tempers vary from sand or plant matter to hair, crushed shells, and crushed pottery. Materials that are naturally present in some clays, such as mica (a mineral), often look like tempers that people have added.

Pottery can be made in a number of ways. Early vessels were handmade. Pottery could also be molded in different types of forms. The potter's wheel was invented in about 4500 B.C.E. Pottery made on a wheel often has recognizable marks that show this.

Firing (oven-baking the pottery until it is hard) is also important. Different temperatures and firing times produce different results. The amount of oxygen in a kiln (pottery oven), can change the color of a vessel from red to black.

The surface areas of the pottery could be treated in different ways. They might be given a thin coat of liquid clay called a slip. After 1500 B.C.E. glazes (glasslike finishes) were also used.

Patterns and designs might be painted on or incised (marked) into the clay using a stick or another tool. Some pots were polished to a shiny finish, a process called burnishing.

▶ A potter makes a vessel using a series of coils that he will build up, either smoothing them with his hand or finishing them on a potter's wheel. Most pottery was wheel-made, but some vessels were molded. Bowls were made by pressing clay into forms. They were very common and may have been used to bake bread. Nearby are the pots which the potter has made and decorated. Some designs were marked on the surface using a sharp instrument. Others were painted with vegetable dyes. The vessels would be fired hard in a pottery kiln (oven).

First Civilization (7000–4000 B.C.E.)

POTTERY USE WAS WIDESPREAD IN WEST Asia by 7000 B.C.E. Distinctive pottery types emerged at different sites, after which the cultures have been named. Most settlements were in the dry-farming zone of rainfall (10 inches/ 25 cm in a year). Over the next 3,000 years village life became more organized, and fields were irrigated.

Early pottery cultures

The rectangular mud-brick houses in the village at Tell Hassuna in northern Iraq had several rooms and courtyards. Pottery was fired in large domed kilns. Clay spindle whorls indicate that wool was woven here. Obsidian, turquoise, and seashells found here point to trade with Anatolia and Sinai.

The Samarra and Choga Mami cultures spread south from Hassuna. Early farmers relied on rainfall to sustain their crops, but in these areas the rainfall alone was not enough. At Choga Mami, water channels show that irrigation was used to bring water to the fields.

▼ Ubaid pottery was decorated with dark painted patterns on a pale background.

▶ An Ubaid female fertility figurine from Ur with an unusual "lizardlike" head.

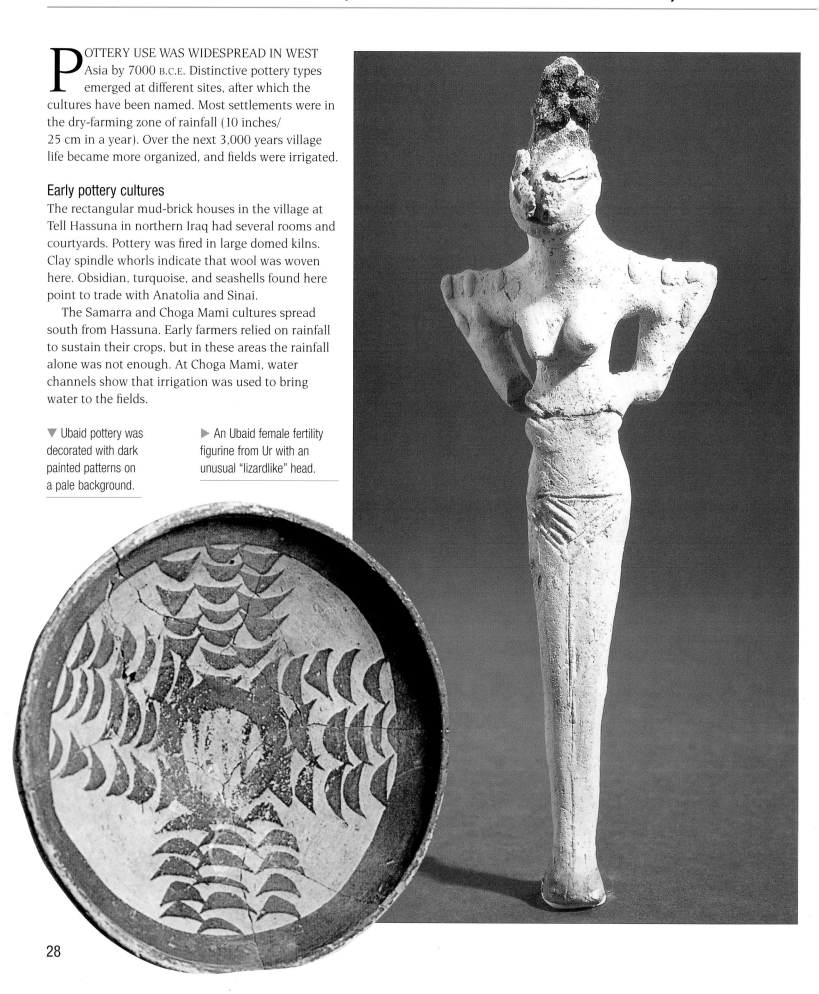

► Finely carved jars and a bowl made from alabaster (a compound of gypsum and water). They were found in graves from the Samarran period excavated at Tell al-Sawwan in central Iraq.

▼ Early pottery cultures, 7000–5400 B.C.E. In about 6000 B.C.E. the Hassuna culture overlapped the Samarra culture. About 1,000 years later the Halaf culture spread through the Zagros Mountains to northern Syria. The Ubaid culture developed in Sumer in southern Mesopotamia.

Pottery cultures, 7000–4000 B.C.E.

Cultures are represented by named archaeological sites.

7000 B.C.E. PROTO-HASSUNA

6800 B.C.E. HASSUNA
    Sites: Hassuna, Iraq; Tell Umm Dabaghiyeh, Iraq

6500 B.C.E. SAMARRA
    Sites: Tell al-Sawwan, Iraq; Choga Mami, Iraq

6000 B.C.E. HALAF (EARLY)
    Sites: Tell Halaf, Syria; Arpachiyeh, Iraq; Yarim Tepe, Iraq

5900 B.C.E. UBAID (EARLY)
    Site: Tell Halaf, Syria

5400 B.C.E. UBAID (LATE)
    Site: Eridu, Iraq

Halaf culture

The Hassuna culture was replaced by the Halaf, named after the site on the Habur River in Syria. People here lived in domed mud-brick round huts called *tholoi*. The Halaf culture produced fine pottery that was painted with intricate and sophisticated patterns. By 5500 B.C.E. the northern Halaf culture came into contact with the Ubaid culture.

Ubaid culture

The Ubaid culture developed in the south of Mesopotamia and lasted for more than 1,000 years. At Eridu in Sumer, a series of temples were built, possibly to the water god Enki. A cemetery was found containing 200 rectangular mud-brick graves. The houses had a central room that was flanked by two rows of rooms.

The distinctively painted pottery from the Late Ubaid has been found in Saudi Arabia, Bahrain, and Qatar. This shows that there was already appreciable trade with the Gulf region.

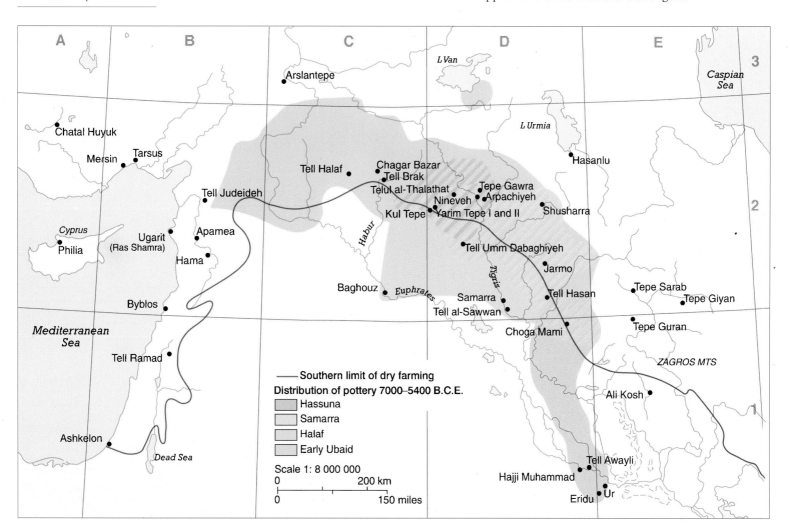

Mesopotamian Sites

Tell Madhhur

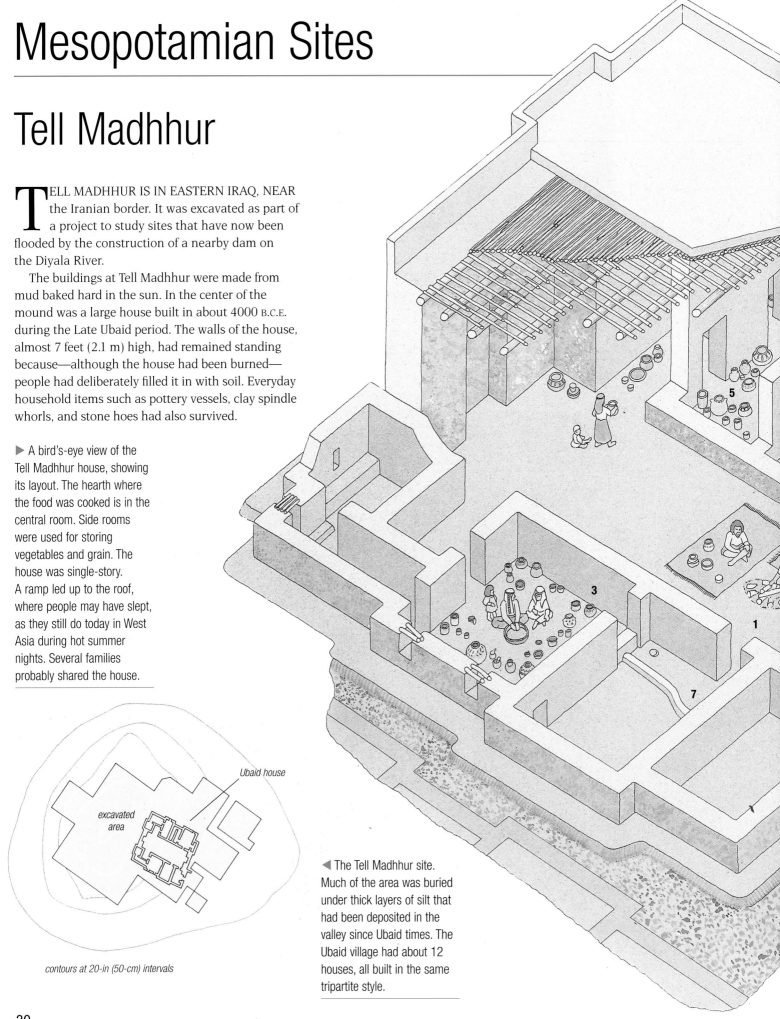

TELL MADHHUR IS IN EASTERN IRAQ, NEAR the Iranian border. It was excavated as part of a project to study sites that have now been flooded by the construction of a nearby dam on the Diyala River.

The buildings at Tell Madhhur were made from mud baked hard in the sun. In the center of the mound was a large house built in about 4000 B.C.E. during the Late Ubaid period. The walls of the house, almost 7 feet (2.1 m) high, had remained standing because—although the house had been burned—people had deliberately filled it in with soil. Everyday household items such as pottery vessels, clay spindle whorls, and stone hoes had also survived.

▶ A bird's-eye view of the Tell Madhhur house, showing its layout. The hearth where the food was cooked is in the central room. Side rooms were used for storing vegetables and grain. The house was single-story. A ramp led up to the roof, where people may have slept, as they still do today in West Asia during hot summer nights. Several families probably shared the house.

excavated area

Ubaid house

contours at 20-in (50-cm) intervals

◀ The Tell Madhhur site. Much of the area was buried under thick layers of silt that had been deposited in the valley since Ubaid times. The Ubaid village had about 12 houses, all built in the same tripartite style.

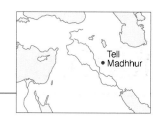

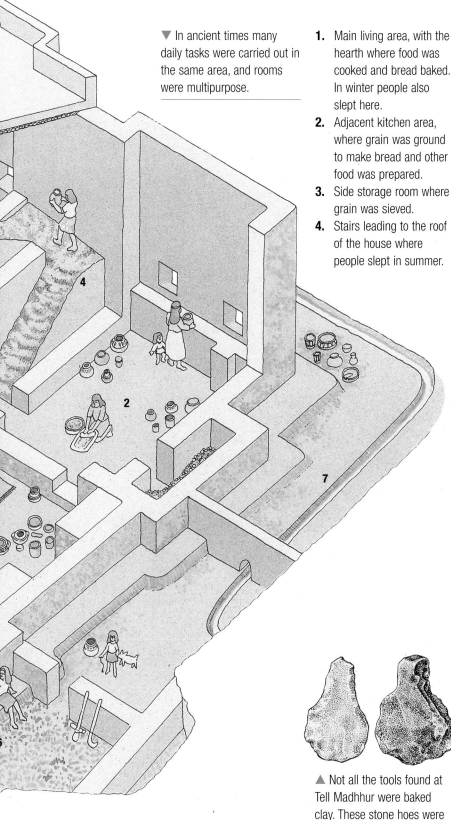

▼ In ancient times many daily tasks were carried out in the same area, and rooms were multipurpose.

1. Main living area, with the hearth where food was cooked and bread baked. In winter people also slept here.
2. Adjacent kitchen area, where grain was ground to make bread and other food was prepared.
3. Side storage room where grain was sieved.
4. Stairs leading to the roof of the house where people slept in summer.
5. Storage rooms for food.
6. Entrance to house.
7. Open drainage channel.

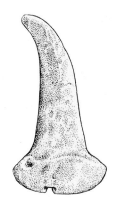

▶ A baked-clay pestle shaped like a bent nail. In the Late Ubaid period many tools were made out of baked clay. They were as strong as stone utensils. Other baked-clay items found at Tell Madhhur include grindstones and spindle whorls.

"Tripartite" architecture

Ubaid houses were built in three parts. A long central room that functioned as the main living area was flanked on each side by several smaller rooms. This design is called "tripartite." Tripartite houses have been found at Ubaid sites such as Tepe Gawra in northern Iraq.

The style also seems to have been used for the design of temples. Three temples at Tepe Gawra were built according to a tripartite plan, as were others in the south, at Eridu and Uruk.

Where this style first came from is not known, but it may have come as the result of trade or contact with people farther south. It became the main form for West Asian temple architecture. People built tripartite temples for almost 2,000 years, from southern Mesopotamia to northern Syria.

▲ Not all the tools found at Tell Madhhur were baked clay. These stone hoes were made of chipped flint. They would have been attached to a wooden handle by bitumen and a cord. Only stone or clay products survived the fire.

▲ Among the 78 pottery items found in the house was this small painted cup or bowl. Pottery of all shapes and sizes was found. Some of the grain-storage jars were enormous and could hold as much as 24 gals (109 l).

▲ A spouted jar, for storing and pouring liquids, was found in the kitchen. Similar vessels have been found at other sites. Most pots in the house were handmade, but some may have been finished on a wheel.

Birth of the City (4000–3000 B.C.E.)

THE FIRST CITIES DEVELOPED IN SOUTHERN Mesopotamia in about 4000 B.C.E. Much earlier, Jericho and Chatal Hüyuk had shown some of the features of cities—including walls and closely spaced housing. But these early sites were unique, and the "urban revolution" only began later in the Uruk period.

The change from village to city life took place between 4300 and 3450 B.C.E. Larger numbers of people began living more closely together, and many of them ceased to be farmers. Religious centers such as temples began to be built.

In the Early and Middle Uruk periods the northern region around Nippur was well populated. In the Late Uruk period most settlements were in southern Mesopotamia. This movement of people may have been caused by the Euphrates River changing its course. In the following Jamdat Nasr and Early Dynastic periods many thousands of people lived in the city of Uruk and its surrounding areas.

Specialized labor

Large urban populations involved a very different social organization from that of villages. Many people became specialists in crafts and trades instead of working as farmers. In the Uruk period large temples were built.

Artistic activity increased throughout the region, reaching Egypt in about 3000 B.C.E. Traders were active, importing lapis lazuli, a blue semiprecious stone, from over 1,250 miles (2,000 km) away in Afghanistan. Copper and its alloys became common and may have been worked by professional smiths. A metal industry was developing, using gold, silver, copper, lead, and iron.

Farmers were using the ox plow by 4000 B.C.E., and their produce may have been carried to the cities in carts pulled by oxen or, in the marshes of southern Mesopotamia, by boat. Records made by scribes of the goods received at Uruk are the earliest known written documents.

▶ Arabs living in the marshes of southern Iraq today use boats for transport. The boats are built from reeds, waterproofed with bitumen, and are similar to boats found at the Royal Cemetery at Ur (about 2600 B.C.E.). Clay models of boats were found in an Ubaid grave at Eridu from about 4000 B.C.E.

▼ Towns of the Late Uruk period. When the Euphrates changed its course, many settlements were abandoned in the north. Large numbers of people moved south, settling nearer Uruk, which was already a big city.

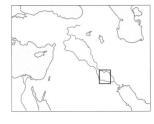

Uruk-based cultures

Cultures are represented by named archaeological sites.

4300–3450 B.C.E. EARLY AND MIDDLE URUK
Sites: Nippur region, Iraq; Uruk, Iraq

3450–3000 B.C.E. LATE URUK
Sites: Uruk, Iraq

3000 B.C.E. JAMDAT NASR
Sites: Uruk, Iraq; Jamdat Nasr, Iraq

▶ Towns of the Early–Middle Uruk period. More than half the population of southern Mesopotamia lived in the fertile alluvial plains to the north and east of Nippur. The Euphrates and Tigris rivers were joined farther upstream.

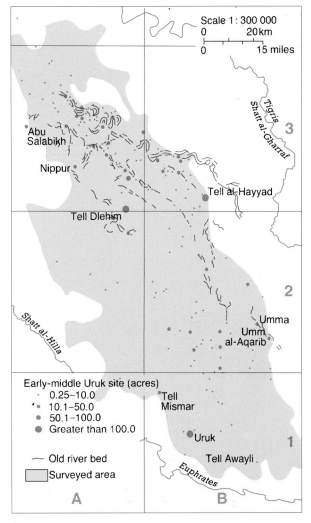

Scale 1 : 300 000

Early-middle Uruk site (acres)
- · 0.25–10.0
- 10.1–50.0
- 50.1–100.0
- ● Greater than 100.0

— Old river bed
Surveyed area

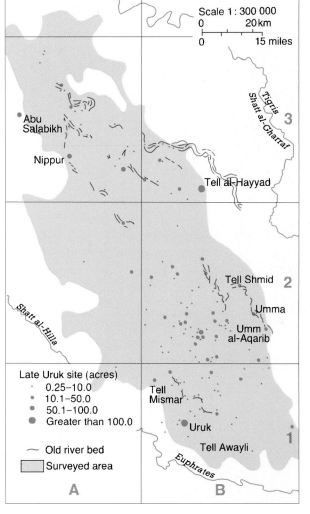

Scale 1 : 300 000

Late Uruk site (acres)
- · 0.25–10.0
- 10.1–50.0
- 50.1–100.0
- ● Greater than 100.0

— Old river bed
Surveyed area

Mesopotamian Sites

Uruk

URUK WAS ONE OF THE MIGHTIEST CITIES in Sumer, southern Mesopotamia, between 4000 B.C.E. and 3000 B.C.E. The site is near modern Warka, 156 miles (250 km) southeast of Baghdad. The Bible mentions Uruk twice: in Genesis, chapter 10 (as Erech), and in Ezra, chapter 4.

Uruk probably developed from two Ubaid settlements—Kullaba and Eanna—where there were temples to the sky god, Anu, and the goddess of love, Inanna. In about 3000 B.C.E. the two sites joined together to form a single city. Uruk covered an area of 1,000 acres (400 ha) and was surrounded by a wall 6 miles (10 km) long.

Gilgamesh, the hero of the great Sumerian story *The Epic of Gilgamesh*, was said to be a king of Uruk.

Temples and their treasures

An important religious site grew up at Uruk, centered on the two temples of Anu and Inanna. The tripartite temples were built on a terrace taking up one-third of the city. Parts of the temples were decorated with

◀ This statuette of an unknown ruler of Uruk dates from the late fourth millennium B.C.E. Such figures were placed in temples as a sign of the ruler's devotion to the gods.

▼ A priestly procession enters the temple precinct at Uruk. The mighty columns of the monumental entrance are over 6 ft (1.8 m) in diameter and are decorated with colored cones stuck into the plaster. A sheep and piles of dates are being brought to the goddess Inanna. The temples were much involved in the way food production was organized.

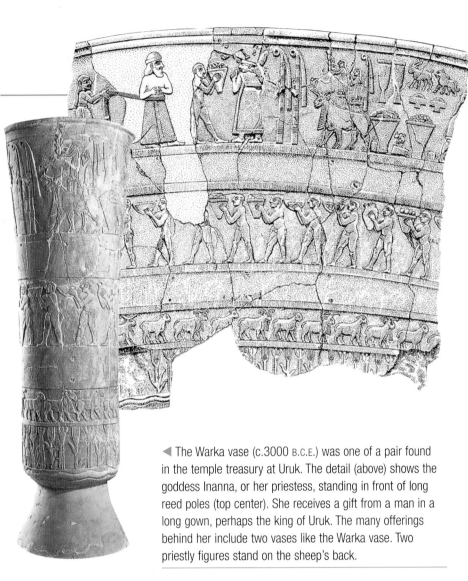

◄ The Warka vase (c.3000 B.C.E.) was one of a pair found in the temple treasury at Uruk. The detail (above) shows the goddess Inanna, or her priestess, standing in front of long reed poles (top center). She receives a gift from a man in a long gown, perhaps the king of Uruk. The many offerings behind her include two vases like the Warka vase. Two priestly figures stand on the sheep's back.

geometric designs made from thousands of stone or clay cones painted red, black, and white. Inside were a stepped altar and a central table for burnt offerings. Staircases on the side led to the roof where particular prayers had to be uttered.

Splendid treasures were found at the sites of these temples. An alabaster vase, more than 3 feet (1 m) high, which is called the Warka vase, has three bands of carving, representing a thanksgiving festival for good harvests to the goddess Inanna. The upper band shows food being offered to Inanna or her priestess. The middle band is a procession of naked men (possibly priests) carrying baskets of produce. The bottom frieze shows sheep and grain heads.

The Warka vase, along with the Mona Lisa of Uruk, a superb life-size mask of a woman's face, was looted from the Iraq Museum in 2003. The Warka vase has fortunately been recovered, but the whereabouts of the Mona Lisa of Uruk is still unknown. This ritual mask, which possibly represents the goddess Inanna, is irreplaceable. Made from white marble, it is almost life-size and probably had semiprecious stones (lapis lazuli) inlaid in the eye sockets.

Cylinder Seals

CYLINDER SEALS ARE SMALL CYLINDER-shaped objects on which a scene or design is carved that leaves a "print" when it is rolled on clay. The design can be reproduced as many times as the cylinder seal is turned. Cylinder seals average 1 inch (2.5 cm) high and 0.6 inches (1.5 cm) in diameter. They were usually made of stone, but metal, ivory, wood, bone, shell, and baked clay were also used. The entire collection of the Iraq Museum was looted in 2003 and has not been recovered.

History of cylinder seals

The earliest cylinder seals that have been found are from Uruk and are dated about 3500 B.C.E. The idea and the use of cylinder seals spread quickly throughout West Asia and as far as Egypt.

Cylinder seals were valuable, especially those made from semiprecious stone, and were probably passed down from one generation to the next. After about 3,000 years, people gradually stopped using seals when alphabetic writing became common.

◀ ▶ A limestone cylinder seal and a drawing of the impression that was made in clay. The metal mount on top is a bull, echoing the cattle design on the seal print.

▼ The *mudhif,* or guest-house, of the Marsh Arabs of southern Iraq is still built of reeds. Its ancient design is shown on cylinder seals from Late Uruk times (3000 B.C.E.).

▼ Many cylinder seals were made of luxury stones, such as lapis lazuli, and worn by their owners as jewelry. The seals were usually pierced lengthwise so that they could be worn on a pin or a piece of string, or mounted on a swivel.

▼ Cylinder seals were made by cutting hard stone with flint or copper tools. When the cylinder had been shaped, the artist would carve the scene or design. Cylinders were pierced with a hand bore to make the hole through which a pin or wire was threaded.

▶ The man on the left of the picture has cut off small lumps of clay, which he is flattening onto pots. He then gives them to the overseer, who rolls a cylinder seal over them to produce a pattern, or impression. When they have set, the seals are attached with rope to the necks of the jars.

◀ ▼ A series of cylinder seal "prints" from different periods. They show animals and mythological creatures. Some of the prints have cuneiform (wedge-shaped writing) inscriptions.

What cylinder seals were used for

Cylinder seals were used to mark the ownership of property. In the case of a storage jar, impressions on a lump of clay would be attached to a string that tied down the cover.

Cylinder seals were needed as a signature or confirmation of receipt. They were often used with cuneiform (wedge-shaped) writing, which had also developed at Uruk. Legal and commercial documents were written on clay tablets and they often show the impression of a cylinder seal engraved with the owner's name.

The cuneiform inscriptions on cylinder seals tell us the names that people had and give us information about family history. Their carved designs often show scenes from daily life, or perhaps highlight the role of the king. Many scenes also illustrate the gods, religious worship, and Mesopotamian mythological stories. People may have believed that their seals had magical properties.

The clay impressions left by the seals provide valuable archaeological evidence. At Jamdat Nasr, north of Uruk, a cylinder-seal print on a clay tablet bore the symbols of the gods of many towns. Similar clay sealings found at Ur in Sumer suggest that there may have been a league of city-states.

Writing

THE EARLIEST KNOWN WRITING COMES from Uruk and has been dated to about 3300 B.C.E. "Word pictures" were drawn with a pointed instrument (known as a stylus) onto tablets of damp clay. Much later the complete system had more than 700 signs. The tablets measured about 2 inches (5 cm) wide and were 0.75 inches (2 cm) thick. Each word picture represented an object. For example, a bull's head meant cattle and an ear of barley meant grain.

Writing developed at Uruk as a convenient way to keep records of produce and accounts of trade. The first tablets that can be read record the transfer of food and other goods. Writing was used first for commerce and later for literature and history.

▲ Cuneiform signs were made by pressing a sharpened reed stylus into clay (right). Most tablets were square, but round ones (left) were used for scribes to learn to write on. It took many years to learn the hundreds of signs.

▲ A cuneiform letter and its envelope. Clay tablets were often put inside such containers. To make sure nobody changed the contents of the letter, identical writing was put on the outside, too.

▲ A hollow clay sphere and tokens. The markings on the sphere may show the number and range of tokens once enclosed inside. Spheres and tokens have been found in southwest Iran and Sumer.

▶ A clay tablet from Uruk inscribed with a very early form of writing. The signs in the lower line may be read as "priest," "prince," and "great." The wedges may be numbers.

Tokens for trade

Tokens developed much earlier than writing. Clay tokens came in various shapes and sizes, perhaps representing different objects. A cone may have meant a bag of wheat, for example, and a disk, a sheep. Later, the symbol for a sheep became a cross inside a circle.

Tokens were placed inside hollow clay spheres (balls) that were then sealed. If one person sent six sheep to another, the sender would put six tokens in the sphere. When the sheep arrived the receiving person would break open the sphere and count the tokens. Then the person would know whether the correct number of sheep had arrived.

The number of tokens also began to be marked on the surface of the sphere. This was probably how writing on clay tablets began.

▶ In the temple warehouse, jars of barley and dates are being stacked by laborers. A temple scribe records amounts of produce on a tablet, while a senior official checks the tablets that are drying on the table. Many early cuneiform documents are lists of food received by temples.

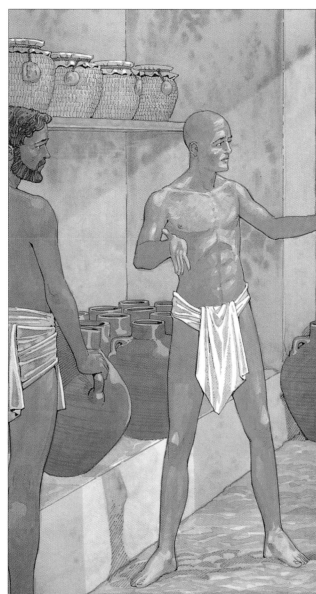

► The main stages in the development of the cuneiform script. The later signs have changed greatly from the original word pictures. This is partly because by 700 B.C.E. the signs had been turned 90 degrees (a right angle). The signs went through many changes of both position and meaning. The Assyrians had a vocabulary of 570 signs, of which 300 were often used.

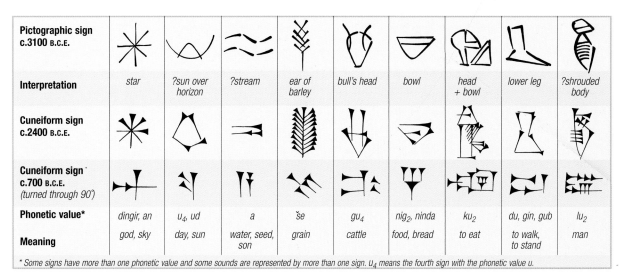

Pictographic sign c.3100 B.C.E.									
Interpretation	star	?sun over horizon	?stream	ear of barley	bull's head	bowl	head + bowl	lower leg	?shrouded body
Cuneiform sign c.2400 B.C.E.									
Cuneiform sign c.700 B.C.E. (turned through 90°)									
Phonetic value*	dingir, an	u_4, ud	a	še	gu_4	nig_2, ninda	ku_2	du, gin, gub	lu_2
Meaning	god, sky	day, sun	water, seed, son	grain	cattle	food, bread	to eat	to walk, to stand	man

* Some signs have more than one phonetic value and some sounds are represented by more than one sign. u_4 means the fourth sign with the phonetic value u.

Cuneiform script

The word pictures written on the tablets at Uruk developed into the script we now call cuneiform. It was a complicated process.

The pictures began to represent ideas and became "ideographs." For example, a bull's head might also mean strength, and the sign of a leg might mean both a person and also to walk. Later the signs became "phonograms," representing sounds as well as the meaning of a picture. The sign of a bull's head now equaled the sound or syllable (a unit of pronunciation of a word) "gu."

Cuneiform (from the Latin *cuneus* = wedge) was a syllabic script with hundreds of wedge-shaped signs that developed from the original pictures.

Who used cuneiform?

Cuneiform was used by many different peoples during its 3,000-year history. The Sumerians were the earliest to write in cuneiform. The Assyrians adopted the script in about 2300 B.C.E., and it was used by the Babylonians, the Elamites in nearby Iran, the Hittites, the Hurrians, and the Urartu who lived in Anatolia. Cuneiform also appears in the Levant at Ugarit, where it was used to write a special alphabet.

Other scripts, such as hieroglyphics (a form of picture writing), were known in Egypt, but cuneiform was the language of politics until the fifth century B.C.E. It died out in the face of Aramaic that emerged in Syria in about 900 B.C.E. With only 22 letters Aramaic was much easier and quicker to write.

Cuneiform continued to be used by some peoples until the first century C.E., but its 900 signs were reduced to about half that number over time.

Sumerian City-States (3000–2350 B.C.E.)

WHEN THE EARLY DYNASTIC I PERIOD replaced the Uruk culture in about 3000 B.C.E., Sumer became a land of city-states. Each state consisted of a city and its lands. There were few physical boundaries in southern Mesopotamia besides the water channels, and city-states fought wars with each other—though they remained mostly independent. The first kings came to power at this time.

The city-state and its leaders

The center of economic wealth in the city-state was the temple. As the home of the patron god or goddess, it was the city's main feature. It owned large areas of land and employed many people. The chief priest was called *en*, or "lord."

The cities had governors called *ensis*. Decisions were made by the free male citizens, probably those who owned land, in a form of democracy. There was

▲ One of more than a dozen known copies of the Sumerian King List. The original, now lost, was written in about 2100 B.C.E.

an upper house of "elders," probably distinguished citizens, and a lower house of "men," perhaps the other landowners. Women did not participate in these assemblies.

In times of crisis, the assembly would elect a leader, called a *lugal*. He was the commander in battles with other city-states. He acted as a judge in disputes and later carried out rituals such as blessing the harvests. He lived in a "great house," or *egal*, a word that came to mean palace or temple.

The *lugal*, or "great man," began to rival the temple in power and wealth. At some point, the position of leader became permanent. Instead of being elected, the *lugal* became a hereditary king. Kings saw themselves as chosen by a "council of the gods"— which met only at the city of Nippur—to carry out the gods' will. Because of this, the Sumerian kings eagerly contributed to the building and maintenance of the religious buildings in the city.

◄ A stone wall plaque from Girsu, in present-day Iraq. Ur-Nanshe, the ruler of Lagash (about 2480 B.C.E.), one of the Sumerian city-states, is shown carrying a basket of bricks on his head. He is acting in his role as the builder of the city and is watched by a female figure who could be a priestess. In the lower part he is seated on his throne with a cup in his hand. The plaque is inscribed in cuneiform, and the hole indicates that it may have been mounted on a pole.

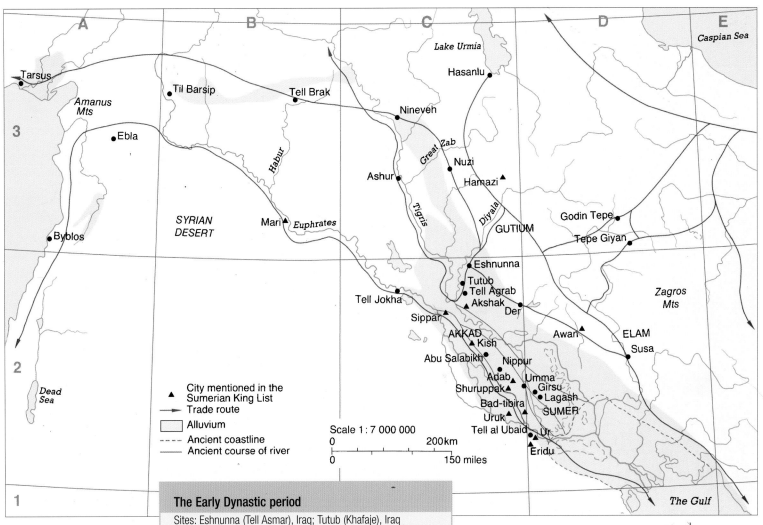

The Early Dynastic period map showing Mesopotamia and surrounding regions.

Map labels:
Tarsus, Amanus Mts, Ebla, Byblos, Dead Sea, Til Barsip, Tell Brak, Habur, SYRIAN DESERT, Mari, Euphrates, Lake Urmia, Hasanlu, Nineveh, Ashur, Great Zab, Nuzi, Hamazi, Tigris, Diyala, GUTIUM, Godin Tepe, Tepe Giyan, Eshnunna, Tutub, Tell Agrab, Akshak, Der, Tell Jokha, Sippar, AKKAD, Kish, Abu Salabikh, Nippur, Awan, ELAM, Susa, Zagros Mts, Adab, Umma, Girsu, Shuruppak, Lagash, Bad-tibira, SUMER, Uruk, Tell al Ubaid, Ur, Eridu, The Gulf, Caspian Sea

Legend:
▲ City mentioned in the Sumerian King List
→ Trade route
Alluvium
--- Ancient coastline
— Ancient course of river

Scale 1 : 7 000 000
0   200km
0   150 miles

▲ Cities in the Sumerian King List. Southern Mesopotamia was divided into two regions. Sumer in the south stretched from Eridu, which was once on the Gulf, to Nippur. The Sumerian King List listed the names of the rulers of the cities of Sumer and the length of their reigns. Reigns were often listed as being very long, even thousands of years. The King List was written to reinforce the idea that kings were linked closely to the gods, who gave assent to their rule. Although not all the facts it states are true, the King List can help us understand history.

The Early Dynastic period

Sites: Eshnunna (Tell Asmar), Iraq; Tutub (Khafaje), Iraq

3000–2750 B.C.E. EARLY DYNASTIC I

2750–2650 B.C.E. EARLY DYNASTIC II

2650–2350 B.C.E. EARLY DYNASTIC III

Ensis of Lagash (2570–2342 B.C.E.)
The ensis of Lagash were not included in the Sumerian King List. Unlike kings, they were not said to have received their position from the gods.

c.2570 B.C.E. En-Hegal

c.2550 B.C.E. Lugal-sha-engur

2494–2465 B.C.E. Ur-Nanshe

2464–2455 B.C.E. Akurgal

2454–2425 B.C.E. E-ana-tum

2424–2405 B.C.E. En-ana-tuma I

2404–2375 B.C.E. En-temena

2374–2365 B.C.E. En-ana-tuma II

2364–2359 B.C.E. En-entar-zi

2358–2352 B.C.E. Lugal-anda

2351–2342 B.C.E. Uru-ku-gina

The Sumerian King List

The Sumerian King List is an ancient cuneiform record of royal rulers. At least 12 copies have been found in Babylonia and Nineveh and at Susa in Iran. It lists all the kings of the Early Dynastic period, many of whom are mentioned in other cuneiform inscriptions. Although the King List places the kings one after the other, they often ruled at the same time at different city-states. The first name on the list that has been authenticated by archaeological finds is Enmebaragesi of Kish.

Sumerian influence

Sumer was divided into a number of small city-states. Its political influence was weak, but Sumerian culture spread throughout West Asia. Sumerian-style statues were found at Ashur. The city of Mari in eastern Syria had strong links with Mesopotamia. At Ebla, in western Syria, 8,000 clay tablets were found written in a Sumerian cuneiform script.

Mesopotamian Sites

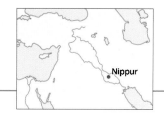

Nippur

LOCATED 100 MILES (160 KM) SOUTH OF Baghdad, Nippur is a huge *tell* (mound) 66 feet (20 m) high, covering an area of about 750 acres (300 ha). People lived at Nippur for more than 5,000 years, until the ninth century C.E. In the Early Dynastic period, the lands of Sumer and Akkad met at this city.

Enlil, the lord of the air, was the main Sumerian god. His temple at Nippur was the most important shrine in Sumer. Sumerians believed it was at Nippur that the gods met in an assembly to elect kings.

Kings of the Third Dynasty of Ur may have lived at Nippur in about 2000 B.C.E., but the city was never the capital of a dynasty. Rulers of other cities thought that control of Nippur, with its religious importance, gave them the right to rule all of Sumer and Akkad.

During the reign of Ur-Nammu (2112–2095 B.C.E.), the first ziggurats, the high temple platforms, were constructed in Mesopotamia. The ziggurat at Nippur was built in about 2100 B.C.E. At the top of this vast tiered structure was Enlil's temple, which was called the *ekur*, or "mountain house." It became the most important shrine (holy place) in Mesopotamia. Near the ziggurat was the temple of Inanna, the Mesopotamian goddess of love and war.

The remains of the ziggurat are still visible, and 100 years ago excavators from the University of Pennsylvania built a dig house on top of the mound to protect themselves from the local warring Arab tribes. The site has been excavated by archaeologists from the University of Chicago, but since 2003 it has suffered much damage by robbers looking for treasures to sell on the illegal antiquities market.

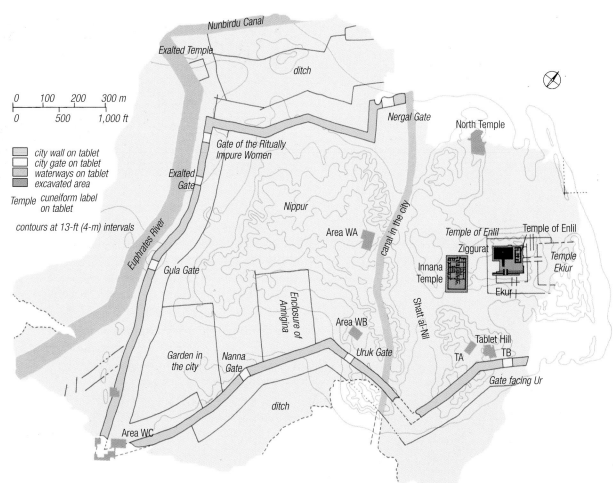

◀ The site of Nippur, including features from a unique scale drawing of the city on a cuneiform tablet dated about 1300 B.C.E. The tablet shows the temple of Enlil, the city walls, the gates, and the main canal. Thousands of cuneiform tablets have been found at Nippur, where there was a famous scribal school. Excavations at the south end of the site have found where the sharp ends of the wall join. In ancient times the Euphrates River flowed by the eastern walls, but later the river changed course.

Ebla

TELL MARDIKH WAS IDENTIFIED AS THE ancient city of Ebla in 1968. Located in Syria, south of Aleppo, people lived at Ebla for more than 3,500 years, until 800 C.E. Its most important period was from 2500 to 1500 B.C.E.

Eight thousand cuneiform texts were discovered at Ebla. They came from the library of what is called "Palace G." Most of the clay tablets were written in Eblaite, a previously unknown local language that is closely related to the language of Akkad. Many of the texts discuss administrative matters. The king was extremely wealthy. He owned 80,000 sheep and received income of 11 pounds (5 kg) of gold and 1,100 pounds (500 kg) of silver each year.

▼ The ancient city of Ebla. The city covered an area of 120 acres (48 ha) and had an enormous royal complex at its heart.

▶ A human-headed golden bull with a stone beard, found in Palace G at Ebla. The figure may be linked to worship of the sun god Shamash. It is Sumerian in style. Later, huge human-headed bulls guarded the entrances to Assyrian palaces.

▼ A gold necklace, dated to about 1750 B.C.E., found in a tomb beneath Ebla's Western Palace. The decoration on the disks was made with tiny gold granules, and the three-section band was made by "coiling." These techniques were developed in Sumer.

▼ Ebla's archive room. From traces left behind after the burning of this room, the original shelving system can be worked out. When the room was discovered, the clay tablets lay where they fell when the wooden shelves collapsed in the city's destruction. Many of the tablets were badly smashed and must be painstakingly pieced together.

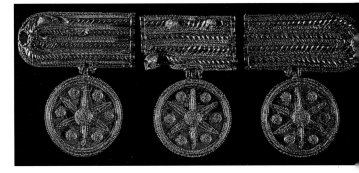

Ebla and Sumer

Ebla had many links with Sumer. Some texts were written in both Eblaite and Sumerian. Delicate gold jewelry found in Palace G had been made using techniques developed in Sumer's Early Dynastic period. A limestone inlay was decorated with battle scenes in typical Sumerian style.

Ebla was a thriving kingdom, at its wealthiest between 2400 and 2250 B.C.E., when the Early Dynastic period ended and the Akkadian rulers came to power. The city's huge royal complex contained a palace, buildings for administration and storage, and workshops. Ebla traded far and wide—from nearby Carchemish to central Anatolia, Ashur in northern Mesopotamia, and Afghanistan. After being attacked by the Mesopotamian king Naram-Sin (2254–2218 B.C.E.) the city never recovered its economic prosperity.

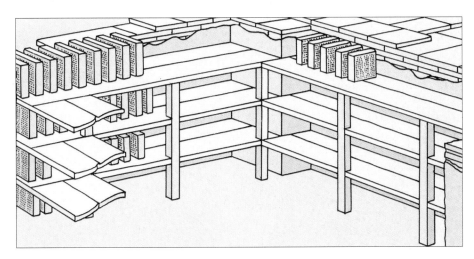

Mesopotamian Sites

Ur

THE ANCIENT CITY OF UR IS IN SOUTHERN Iraq. It was founded during the Ubaid period in about 4000 B.C.E. when people also first settled in Sumer.

Ur was near the Euphrates River, and some of the city's earliest remains were covered with heavy silt from it. This may be evidence of a terrible flood, memories of which were handed down and recorded in the Bible (Genesis, chapters 6–8).

Genesis, chapter 11, claimed Ur as the home of the Hebrew patriarch Abraham. This city was also a port for trade with the Gulf until 1700 B.C.E.

The main temple was dedicated to the moon god Nanna. Ur was abandoned in about 300 B.C.E., probably as a result of floods.

▲ Two lyres as they were found in the tomb of Queen Puabi. A number of stone and metal vessels were found near the lyres, together with the bodies of 10 women wearing fine jewelry. The hands of one woman were still touching one of these musical instruments, at the place where the strings would have been.

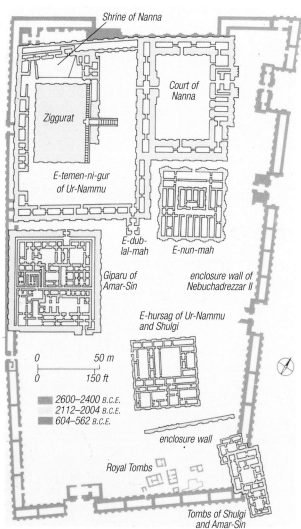

Shrine of Nanna
Court of Nanna
Ziggurat
E-temen-ni-gur of Ur-Nammu
E-dub-lal-mah
E-nun-mah
Giparu of Amar-Sin
enclosure wall of Nebuchadrezzar II
E-hursag of Ur-Nammu and Shulgi

| 0 | 50 m |
| 0 | 150 ft |

- 2600–2400 B.C.E.
- 2112–2004 B.C.E.
- 604–562 B.C.E.

enclosure wall

Royal Tombs

Tombs of Shulgi and Amar-Sin

◀ The sacred enclosure with the temple and the ziggurat of Nanna, the moon god. It was built by the kings of the Third Dynasty of Ur (2112–2004 B.C.E.). Ur-Nammu, Shulgi, and Amar-Sin also seem to have lived and been buried here. The royal tombs were inside the walls.

▼ Gaming boards similar to this one were found in the royal tombs. They were made from pieces of shell, bone, lapis lazuli, and red limestone set into various patterns. Two sets of seven counters were used to play the game, but the exact rules are unknown.

▲ An exquisitely worked gold dagger (with lapis lazuli handle) and sheath. The Sumerian goldsmiths were masters of their craft. The sheath was decorated in fine granules of gold.

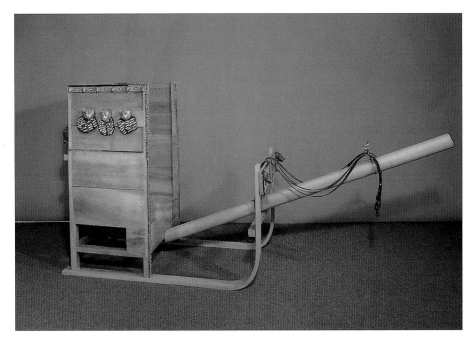

The royal cemetery at Ur

Excavations in the 1920s at Ur uncovered more than 1,000 graves from the end of the Early Dynastic period (2400–2350 B.C.E.). Spectacular treasures were found, including the so-called Standard of Ur, a delicately inlaid box with a banquet scene on one side and a war procession on the other. Together with many other finds from the royal cemetery at Ur, it is now in the British Museum (*see pages 22 and 50*).

Inscriptions identify the royal graves of King Meskalamdug and Queens Puabi and Ninbanda. Mass burials suggest that human sacrifice took place—some kings and queens were buried with their servants, who seem to have died by drinking poison or taking a drug.

▲ Reconstructed wooden sled from the tomb of Queen Puabi. Two oxen were still attached to the sled in the tomb. The reins went through a silver ring decorated with a donkey made from electrum (a gold/silver alloy).

▲ A stone weight shaped like a duck, found at Ur. The inscription gives its weight as "5 minas for Nanna." A mina weighed about 1 lb (0.5 kg).

▶ A superb electrum helmet from the tomb of King Meskalamdug. The Sumerians could dissolve silver from the surface of the alloy so that it would look like gold. The finely fashioned hair is held in place by a diadem suggesting a royal owner.

Ziggurats

LOOKING VERY IMPRESSIVE AGAINST THE FLAT Mesopotamian landscape, pyramid-shaped ziggurats symbolized sacred mountains and were first built in about 2000 B.C.E.

People had already built temples on platforms at Eridu in the Ubaid period, and ziggurats were similar religious buildings. They appeared with the revival of Sumerian rule after the dynasty of Akkad (2334–2154 B.C.E.). King Ur-Nammu of the Third Dynasty of Ur constructed ziggurats at Ur, Eridu, Uruk, and Nippur.

Design of the ziggurat at Ur

The ziggurat at Ur had a rectangular base with three staircases that met at right angles and went up to two more stages to reach the high temple. The ziggurat core was made of mud-bricks, but burned bricks with a bitumen mortar were used for the outside. Many bricks were stamped with Ur-Nammu's name. Drains carried off the water from the upper parts.

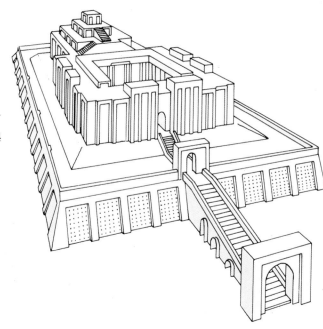

◄ The ziggurat at Tell al-Rimah was built by Shamshi-Adad I in about 1800 B.C.E. The ziggurat was part of the temple building, and the upper shrine was probably reached from the roof of the courtyard temple.

The ziggurat of Babylon

Ziggurats were built throughout southern and northern Mesopotamia and also in Elam. When Babylon became the center of religious worship, its ziggurat became more famous than the one at Ur. This ziggurat stood for 1,000 years, until Sennacherib demolished it in 689 B.C.E. Dedicated to Marduk, the main god of Babylon, the ziggurat became identified with the biblical tower of Babel (Genesis, chapter 11).

Herodotus, the Greek historian, described the ziggurat at Babylon as having six levels crowned by a temple. Its dimensions were also given in a Babylonian clay tablet. The ziggurat was called Etemenanki, which means "the temple of the foundation of heaven and earth."

▼ Building a ziggurat involved hundreds of laborers. Some laborers carry mud-bricks, which are being made nearby. Others carry reeds that will be woven into matting to be placed between the layers of bricks.

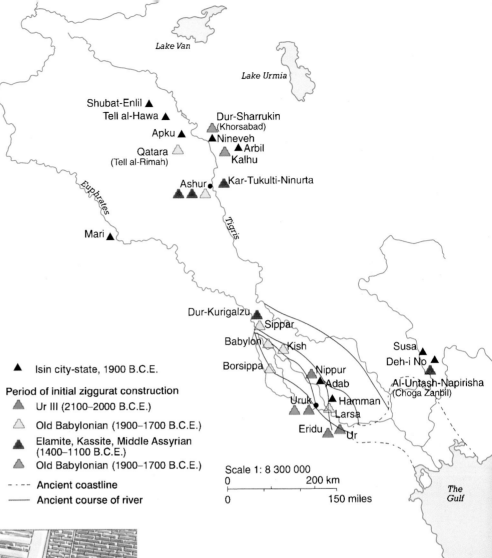

▲ Isin city-state, 1900 B.C.E.

Period of initial ziggurat construction
▲ Ur III (2100–2000 B.C.E.)
△ Old Babylonian (1900–1700 B.C.E.)
▲ Elamite, Kassite, Middle Assyrian (1400–1100 B.C.E.)
▲ Old Babylonian (1900–1700 B.C.E.)
- - - Ancient coastline
——— Ancient course of river

Scale 1: 8 300 000

0   200 km

0   150 miles

▲ Ziggurats of Mesopotamia. Ziggurats have been excavated at 16 sites. Others are known from the shape of the mound or from literature. Dur-Sharrukin was one of the first excavated.

▼ Ziggurats look like the stepped pyramids in Egypt (top), which were tombs. Stepped temples are found in Central America (bottom), but there was no contact with Mesopotamia.

Religion and Ritual

ACCORDING TO MESOPOTAMIAN RELIGION, human beings were created to serve the gods. Each city had a patron god, and these gods lived in images in the temples dedicated to them. The priests and other people who worked at the temples were their servants. Kings were thought to be appointed by the will of the gods.

Mesopotamian gods

Anu, the sky god, was the chief Sumerian god. He reigned over the heavens and lived in the uppermost region, which was called "the sky of Anu." Anu's city was Uruk, which also housed the famous Eanna temple complex of Inanna, goddess of love and war. Enlil, the "lord of the wind," whose city was Nippur, was the son of Anu. He replaced his father as the main god. Enki, god of living water, had his temple at Eridu. Ur was the city of Nanna, the moon god. Temples at Larsa and Sippar were built for the sun god Utu.

By 2000 B.C.E., the Sumerian gods became combined with the Akkadian gods and took their names. Inanna became Ishtar. Shamash, which literally meant "sun," replaced Utu. Nanna was now called Sin. In Babylonian times, Marduk became the chief god, with his temple at Babylon.

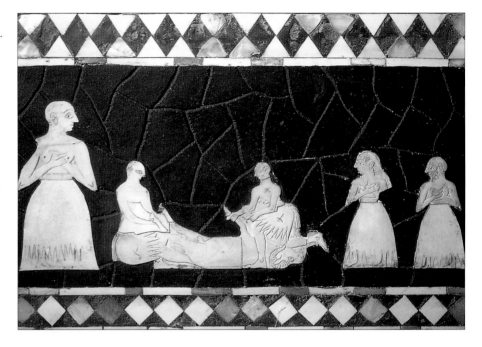

▲ Priests slaughtering a ram. Animal sacrifices were common and could involve large numbers of sheep. The intestines would be examined for omens about the future.

▶ Drawings of seal impressions in clay, found at Ashur. The dog was the symbol of the goddess Gula. The goat-fish was linked with Ea, god of waters.

◀ A group of Sumerian statues from Eshnunna. They are not gods, but represent worshipers and were placed in the temples to pray for the life of the person who gave them. The hands are clasped in prayer. Some of the eyes, inlaid with bitumen and shell, are still intact. Each person was believed to have a special god or goddess who would protect them from demons.

Images of the gods and demons

The Mesopotamians thought that their gods looked and behaved like people but had supernatural powers. A very large number of images of gods and goddesses have been found, from statues to wall plaques. Cylinder seals and other pieces of art show gods and goddesses with human bodies. The gods were shown with beards. To signal that they were different from people, images of the gods and goddesses always included a distinctive multitiered horned crown or helmet and a seven-petaled rosette engraved near the head.

Gods and goddesses also had their own symbols. The crescent and circle represented Sin, the moon god. The star was Ishtar's sign. Sometimes the gods held their symbols in their hands. At other times the divine symbols sprouted from their shoulders. The images of the gods and goddesses often changed throughout Mesopotamian history.

Besides the gods, people in West Asia believed in supernatural spirits and demons, both good and bad. Many of these took half-human and half-animal forms. Some demons were thought to cause diseases and other misfortunes, which superstitious people took complicated precautions to avoid.

▲ Ur-Nammu, king of Ur between 2112 and 2095 B.C.E., makes a libation (drink offering) to the moon god Sin. Sin is seated on a throne, holding in his hand a rod, a ring, and possibly a necklace. Water, beer, oil, wine, and blood were used for libations.

▶ A bronze statue of the king of the evil wind demons, Pazuzu. He is shown with grotesque face, four wings, bird's legs, animal paws, and a scorpion's tail. Demons such as Pazuzu were not always evil and sometimes protected people from other demons.

Part Two

Kingdoms and Empires

▲ A cuneiform tablet from the royal library at Nineveh, recording observations of the stars and planets. Assyrian kings employed expert astrologers.

▶ Detail from the "war" side of the "Standard of Ur," found in the Royal Cemetery at Ur. It shows the victorious troops of Ur, on foot or in chariots. Four mules pull the empty chariot (top left) of the king .

Kings of Agade (2350–2000 B.C.E.)

MESOPOTAMIA BECAME UNITED WHEN Sargon of Akkad conquered both the northern and southern regions of Mesopotamia. The Akkadian language was now spoken rather than Sumerian, and Mesopotamian rule extended throughout West Asia.

Sargon of Agade

Sargon was the first king of the dynasty of Agade and he ruled for 56 years. His name in Akkadian meant "the true king," but his origins were humble. The Sumerian King List states that his father was a date-grower, and another account says that he was a gardener favored by the goddess Ishtar. He grew to become the royal cup-bearer at the court of Kish.

Sargon built a new capital city at Agade, which was probably near Babylon. He conquered the city-states of Uruk, Ur, Umma, and Lagash in southern Mesopotamia, and he was also called the King of Kish and King of the Land.

▼ The kings of Agade conquered an empire that stretched from the Mediterranean to modern Iran. Sargon claimed that he ruled the whole world "from the sunrise to the sunset." This boast could have been a later tradition. From their widespread territories, the kings of Agade obtained such raw materials as wood from Lebanon and silver from Anatolia.

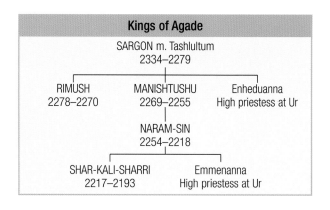

Kings of Agade

SARGON m. Tashlultum
2334–2279

| RIMUSH 2278–2270 | MANISHTUSHU 2269–2255 | Enheduanna High priestess at Ur |

NARAM-SIN
2254–2218

| SHAR-KALI-SHARRI 2217–2193 | Emmenanna High priestess at Ur |

Sargon's sons

Rimush and Manishtushu, Sargon's sons, carried on their father's military campaigns. They took Akkadian rule as far north as Ashur and Nineveh and also east into the Elamite territories. Talking about his conquests of the distant regions Anshan and Sherihum, now in Iran, Manishtushu said: "It is absolutely true!"

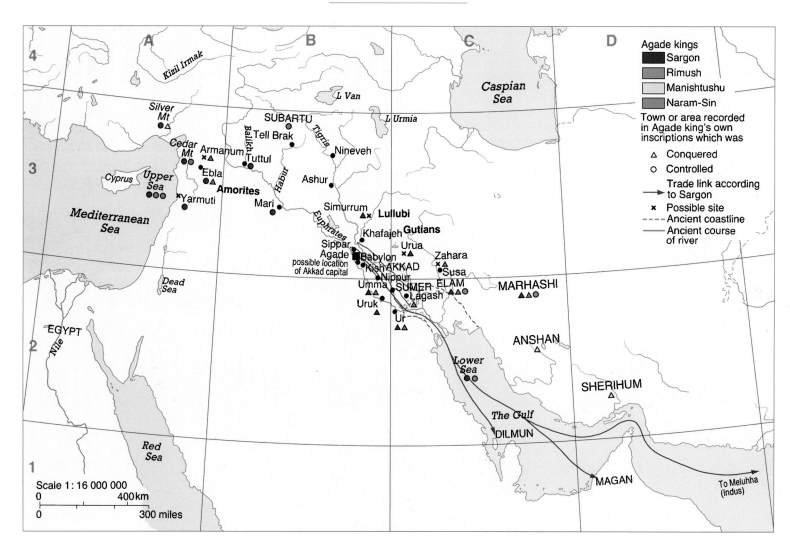

▶ A limestone statue of Gudea, the ruler of Lagash, who wears a fur headdress. He is holding a vase from which flow two streams of living water, symbolized by the fish.

▼ This superb life-size head was made from copper. It is hollow, but the eyes would have been inlaid with stones. The beard, hair, and diadem indicate a king, possibly Sargon or Naram-Sin.

Naram-Sin

Naram-Sin, Sargon's grandson, ruled for 37 years and called himself King of the Universe. His empire extended from Susa in the east to Ebla on the Mediterranean coast. He claimed to be a god, and he made people address him as "god of Agade." Inscriptions show his name marked with the sign that was used to indicate gods.

Naram-Sin was followed by his son, Shar-kali-sharri, who reigned for 17 years. But the empire of Agade began to collapse because of internal problems and pressure from the Gutians, who came from the Zagros Mountains. The city of Agade was sacked and has never been found.

The Third Dynasty of Ur

With the downfall of the Akkadian empire, Sumerian rule revived once more. At Ur, King Ur-Nammu built the famous ziggurat as well as other temples and a palace. Ur-Nammu's power was concentrated in southern Mesopotamia, for he also controlled Eridu and Uruk and erected buildings at Nippur and Larsa. One of his sons married a daughter of the king of Mari, linking the two nations.

Shulgi, Ur-Nammu's son, reigned for 47 years after his father's death. Like Naram-Sin he also claimed he was a god. Shulgi carried on the building work begun by his father and expanded the kingdom eastward and northward to Ashur and Susa. He introduced many reforms during his reign, making the governors (ensis) and military commanders (shagins) report directly to him.

Shulgi controlled the temple lands, reorganized the system of weights, introduced a new calendar, established a code of law, and imposed new taxes. In just one year alone 28,000 cattle and 350,000 sheep passed through Puzrish-Dagan, which was a redistribution center for taxes located a few miles south of Nippur.

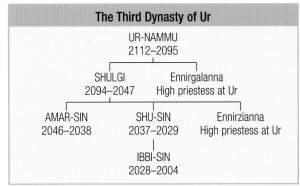

The Third Dynasty of Ur

UR-NAMMU
2112–2095

SHULGI   Ennirgalanna
2094–2047   High priestess at Ur

AMAR-SIN   SHU-SIN   Ennirzianna
2046–2038   2037–2029   High priestess at Ur

IBBI-SIN
2028–2004

Rival Kingdoms (2000–1600 B.C.E.)

IN ABOUT 2000 B.C.E. THE THIRD DYNASTY of Ur broke up into several smaller kingdoms. This marked the end of a united Mesopotamia.

Following the breakup of Mesopotamia, the two most important new kingdoms were Isin and Larsa, after which this period in Mesopotamian history has been named. The most famous king was Rim-Sin of Larsa, who reigned from 1822 to 1763 B.C.E. In 1804 B.C.E. he defeated Uruk and 10 years later he captured Isin.

New peoples arrived in Mesopotamia and began to settle among the Akkadian and Sumerian communities. The Amorites—nomads from the Arabian desert region who spoke a Semitic language—became powerful in the kingdoms of Babylon, Kish, and Larsa.

Large numbers of Hurrians, who spoke an Indo-European language, came from Anatolia into northern Mesopotamia and western Syria. Texts from Alalakh on the Orontes River in Syria show that almost half the population there had Hurrian names.

Kingdoms of Mesopotamia, 2025–1595 B.C.E.

Selected outstanding kings are listed for each kingdom.

First Dynasty of Isin, 2017–1794 B.C.E.
Isme-Dagan (1953–1935 B.C.E.)
Lipit-Ishtar (1934–1924 B.C.E.)

Larsa Dynasty, 2025–1763 B.C.E.
Rim-Sin I (1822–1763 B.C.E.)

1763 B.C.E. Rim Sin I defeated by Hammurabi, ending the Larsa dynasty

First Dynasty of Babylon, 1894–1595 B.C.E.
Hammurabi (1792–1750 B.C.E.)

Asur
Shamshi-Adad I (c. 1813–1781 B.C.E.)
Ishme-Dagan I (1780–1741 B.C.E.)

Mari
Zimri-Lim (1779–1757 B.C.E.)

1757 B.C.E. Zimri-Lim defeated by Hammurabi, and the kingdom of Mari ends

▼ City-states of the Isin and Larsa period. The rival states that followed the Third Dynasty of Ur were often at war with each other. In 1936 B.C.E. (*left*) Isin was the largest. Twenty-six years later, in 1910 B.C.E., it included only Nippur. The southern cities of Ur and Eridu were still ruled by Larsa in 1802 B.C.E. (*right*), while in the north Babylon had become a major kingdom.

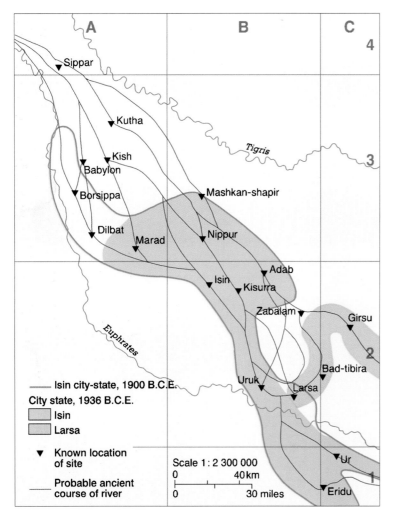

Isin city-state, 1900 B.C.E.

City state, 1936 B.C.E.
- Isin
- Larsa

▼ Known location of site

Probable ancient course of river

Scale 1 : 2 300 000
0   40km
0   30 miles

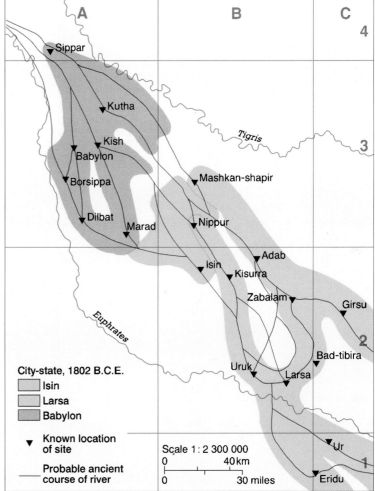

City-state, 1802 B.C.E.
- Isin
- Larsa
- Babylon

▼ Known location of site

Probable ancient course of river

Scale 1 : 2 300 000
0   40km
0   30 miles

◀ A lapis lazuli necklace from a tomb in Kish. The blue semiprecious stone was mined in Afghanistan. The long red carnelian beads are typical of the Harappan culture of the Indus valley. These semiprecious stones were imported.

Trade in the south

The southern Mesopotamian kingdoms competed for the rich trade with the Gulf and beyond. They exported silver, oils, textiles, and barley in exchange for copper, gold, ivory, lapis lazuli, pearls, and other goods. Copper was imported from Magan (modern Oman). Beads found in Mesopotamia show links with the Harappan culture of the Indus valley (Pakistan). Many goods were shipped through Dilmun (probably present-day Bahrain), which was an important trade link between cultures.

▼ A donkey caravan at the *karum* (merchant suburb) outside Kanesh, an important trade center in Anatolia. Donkeys have arrived from Ashur, bringing textiles and tin from Iran. Other donkeys are being loaded to continue farther west. One of the merchants is watching his scribe count the goods.

Trade and conquest in the north

The kingdoms of northern Mesopotamia also traded. Ashur, on the Tigris River, was an important center with a large merchant colony dealing in wool, textiles, and tin. Tin was used to make bronze, instead of copper, for weapons and other goods. It was mined in Iran and Afghanistan and transported by donkey caravans to Kanesh in central Turkey.

Shamshi-Adad, an Amorite, captured many of the northern kingdoms, including Ashur. His lands stretched from the Zagros Mountains to Mari, on the Euphrates River (now in Syria). He claimed to have set up a stele, or pillar, inscribed with his name "in the country of Laban" (that is, Lebanon).

It was the strong personality of Shamshi-Adad that held this Amorite empire together. After his death the reign passed to his two sons who failed to keep control, and so the empire split up. In some places the old kings were restored. In Mari, Zimri-Lim returned to his throne until 1757 B.C.E., when he was conquered by Hammurabi, king of Babylon.

Law and Society

MESOPOTAMIAN KINGS WERE VERY concerned to rule justly. Ur-Nammu of Ur (2112–2095 B.C.E.) wrote the first known law code in the world. His son, Shulgi of Ur, also produced a law code, as did Lipit-Ishtar of Isin and Dadusha of Eshnunna. The most famous code to have survived is that of King Hammurabi, who ruled Babylon from 1792 to 1750 B.C.E.

Hammurabi's law code

Hammurabi's law code is carved on a basalt stele 71.5 feet (22 m) high. The opening words record the king's wish "to cause justice to prevail in the land, to destroy the wicked and the evil, that the strong may not oppress the weak."

The law code may not have been used in courts to decide cases, but the 282 sections contained in it cover many subjects, especially property and commercial law. If one person wronged another, financial compensation—in the form of a sum of silver—was often paid, as had been the custom under Sumerian law.

The idea of punishment that is found in the Old Testament, explained as "Life for life, eye for eye, tooth for tooth, hand for hand, foot for foot" (Deuteronomy, chapter 19, verse 21), can also be found in Hammurabi's code.

◀ This statue, made from diorite, a hard black stone, is thought to be of Hammurabi. He is shown on his law code stele wearing a similar type of headdress. Babylonian kings between 2100 and 1700 B.C.E. wore the same type of royal apparel. The statue was found at Susa in modern Iran, where it had been taken as war booty in the twelfth century B.C.E.

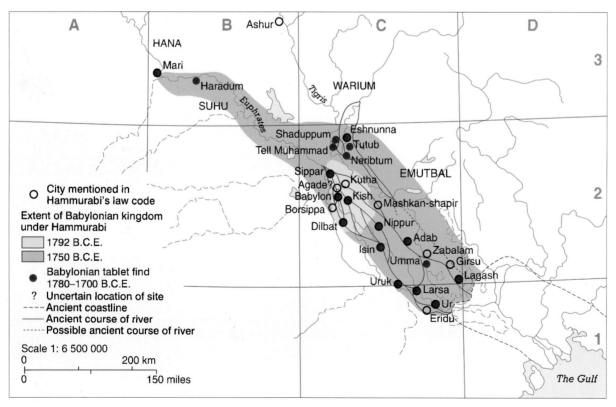

◀ Hammurabi's kingdom. Hammurabi ruled over Mesopotamia only in the second part of his long reign (1792–1750 B.C.E.). He captured Isin and Uruk in 1787 B.C.E. Later, in 1763 B.C.E., with the help of the kings of Mari and Eshnunna, he conquered his long-standing rival, Rim-Sin I of Larsa. In 1761 B.C.E. Hammurabi defeated Mari and in 1755 B.C.E. he was victorious over Eshnunna.

Babylonian society

Hammurabi's law code divides Babylonian society into three social classes: *awilum* (the Akkadian word meaning "man"), *mushkenum*, and *wardum*.

The *awilum* were "freemen" who may also have been landowners. They may have had to pay taxes and perform military service in the royal army. The *mushkenum* could speak in the assembly of "freemen" but they probably did not own property. The *wardum* were slaves. All three classes were, of course, ruled by the king.

When an *awilum* died, his property was divided among his sons. If he fell into debt or could not pay his taxes to the king, he might sell himself, his wife, or his children as slaves.

The king used slaves to build roads, dig canals, and perform other duties. Slaves were expensive to buy, so few were privately owned. Most farms were worked by tenants, who gave a portion of their harvest to the landowner in return for food, animals, and other daily requirements.

Penalties under Hammurabi's code

Many breaches of Hammurabi's law code were punishable by death, even crimes that are not considered as serious in today's society. The code applied different penalties for the same crime, depending on the social class of offender and also of the victim.

If the victim was an *awilum*, the person accused of the crime was punished in the same way as the way in which they had hurt the victim. Law 196, for example, stated that "If an *awilum* has put out the eye of a *mar-awilum* (the son of an *awilum*), they shall put out his eye." (This is known as retributive punishment—the punishment "fits" the crime.)

If the victim was either a *mushkenum* or a *wardum*, a sum of money would be paid instead. Law 198 states: "If an *awilum* has put out the eye of a *mushkenum* or broken his bone, he shall pay one mina of gold."

The idea of retribution—"an eye for an eye"—was not found in Sumerian law and was probably introduced into Mesopotamia by the Amorites. Financial compensation is still practiced in the Middle East today to settle lawsuits.

▶ The stele of Hammurabi's law code from about 1760 B.C.E. The upper part of the basalt pillar shows the king in prayer before Shamash, the sun god and god of justice (seated). Shamash is winged and is wearing the divine horned crown.

Mittani and the Assyrians

IN NORTHERN MESOPOTAMIA AND THE Levant, the kingdom of Mittani became the major power by about 1500 B.C.E. The people of Mittani were Hurrians. (Hurrians were a large ethnic group in the region. The Hurrian language was very different from other West Asian tongues.) Their rulers had Indo-European connections and worshiped ancient Indian gods.

The Mittanians used a new military weapon: the horse-drawn two-wheeled chariot. Washukanni, their capital city, was probably located in present-day northern Syria.

Warfare with Egypt

Egypt was united by Ahmose, the founder of the eighteenth dynasty. In this New Kingdom period Egyptian pharaohs conquered much of the Levant and Palestine—many sites show signs of massive destruction. Pharaoh Amenophis II (1427–1401 B.C.E.) led an army into Mittanian territory and captured the city of Qadesh on the Orontes River.

▼ The empire of Mittani in about 1500 B.C.E. The empire stretched east from Assyria to the Levant. Washukanni, the capital city, has not been positively identified, but may be Tell al-Fakhariyeh in northern Syria. The region around the upper part of the Habur River was the heartland of the empire. Mittanian documents have also been found nearby at Tell Brak.

The Amarna letters

The only written information about the Mittanians comes from foreign sources. The Amarna letters, a collection of 350 clay tablets from Tell Amarna in Egypt, give many details about the government of the Egyptian New Kingdom's territories. They also record diplomatic exchanges between the pharaohs of Egypt and the rulers of independent countries, including Mittani.

Treaties between different states were often cemented through marriage between the rulers' families, and there were many foreign princesses in the harems of the pharaohs. Documents show that royal marriage negotiations were often extremely complicated and drawn out. Tuthmosis IV (1401–1391 B.C.E.) asked the king of Mittani, Artatama, no fewer than seven times for the hand of his daughter before his wish was granted. This marriage of convenience was probably made in an attempt to block the growing power of the Hittites and the Assyrians.

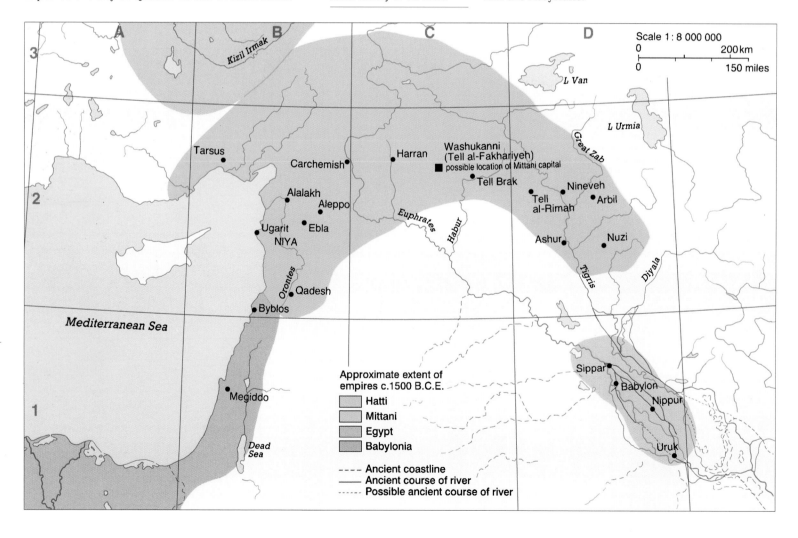

▲ One of the 350 letters from Tell Amarna in central Egypt which record the political history of the pharaohs Amenophis III and Akhenaten. These clay tablets were written in cuneiform, using Akkadian, the international language of the time. Many of the letters describe the situation in Palestine. In the letter shown here, the ruler of Amurru explains why he did not receive the pharaoh's envoy in person.

The Hittites and Assyrians

Hattusas in Anatolia, located in the bend of the Halys River, was the capital of the Hittites. The Hittites were rivals of the Mittanians for control of their lands, and they ended Hammurabi's dynasty when Mursilis I (1626–1595 B.C.E.) overran Babylon.

The Hittites had peaceful relations with the Egyptian pharaohs. The Hittite king Suppiluliumas I made an alliance with the Assyrian powers and married his daughter to the king of Babylon. His victories in Anatolia, the Levant, and northern Mesopotamia reduced the lands held by Mittani, which had grown weaker.

The Assyrian king Adad-nirari (1305–1274 B.C.E.) captured Washukanni and made its ruler, Shattuara, his vassal (junior ruler). The Mittanian kingdom came to an end when it was annexed by Adad-nirari's son Shalmaneser I (1273–1244 B.C.E.). The Assyrians and the Hittites were now the most important powers in Mesopotamia.

▲ A statue of king Idrimi of Alalakh, in northern Syria, who was a vassal of the Mittanian rulers. The seated king's hand on his breast shows his allegiance. Details about his life are given in a cuneiform inscription covering most of his body.

The Kassites (1600–1200 B.C.E.)

THE BABYLONIAN KING LIST RECORDS THAT there were 36 Kassite kings of Babylon, covering a period of several hundred years. After the Hittites conquered the city in 1595 B.C.E., Babylon was governed by the Kassites for four centuries, from the end of the fifteenth until the twelfth century B.C.E. The Kassites may have come originally from Central Asia. They did not speak a Semitic language, and only 48 Kassite words have been identified. Some of them are technical terms for horses—and the Kassites were also noted for their horsemanship. When the Kassites first arrived in Babylon they were agricultural workers. Later, even when their kings ruled Babylon, the Kassites do not appear to have been a large group.

Dur-Kurigalzu

The Kassites rebuilt and restored temples at Ur, Uruk, and Isin. But the best-preserved example of their work is at the site of Agar Quf near Baghdad, which was called Dur-Kurigalzu.

This site was a city built to defend the kingdom against Assyria and Elam. The city was a large one, covering about 495 acres (200 ha). There was a palace as well as a ziggurat (which still stands today), measuring 188 feet (57 m) in height. Dur-Kurigalzu was a major city, but the Kassites regarded Babylon as the capital of their empire and also its religious and commercial center.

Kassite Kings	
Kara-indash	c.1415
Kadashman-Harbe I	
Kurigalzu I	
Kadashman-Enlil I	1374–1360
Burna-Buriash II	1359–1333
Kara-hardash	1333
Nazi-bugash	1333
Kurigalzu II	1332–1308
Nazi-maruttash	1307–1282
Kadashman-Turgu	1281–1264
Kadashman-Enlil II	1263–1255
Kudur-Enlil	1254–1246
Shagarakti-shuriash	1245–1233
Kashtiliash IV	1232–1225
Tulkulli-Ninurta	1224–1216
Enlil-nadin-shumi	1224
Kadashman-Harbe II	1223–1222
Adad-shuma-iddina	1221–1216
Adad-shuma-usur	1215–1186
Melishipak	1185–1171
Marduk-apla-iddina I	1170–1158
Zababa-shuma-iddina	1157
Enlil-nadin-ahi	1156–1154

The Kassite Dynasty, c.1570–1154 B.C.E.

Selected Kassite kings. (Other rulers from the same period are shown in parentheses.)

c.1570 B.C.E. Agum II
c.1510 B.C.E. Burna-Buriash I

c.1390 B.C.E. Kurigalzu I
(Amenophis III of Egypt)

1359–1333 B.C.E. Burna-Buriash II

1332–1308 B.C.E. Kurigalzu II
(Akhenaten of Egypt)

1263–1255 B.C.E. Kadashman-Enlil II
(Hattusilis III, Hittite king)

1232–1225 B.C.E. Kashtiliash IV
Assyrian king Tukulti-Ninurta sacks Babylon

1170–1158 B.C.E. Marduk-apla-iddina
1156–1154 B.C.E. Enlil-nadin-ahi

▼ The Kassite kingdom in the thirteenth century B.C.E. This was an empire that covered most of southern Mesopotamia. It bordered Elam in the east, (now modern Iran) and the Assyrian territories in the north. The Elamites overran the Kassite kingdom in the mid-twelfth century B.C.E. They took back some of the war booty from Babylon, including Hammurabi's law code stele and Naram-Sin's victory stele, to their capital city Susa. The booty was discovered there in the nineteenth century by members of a French expedition.

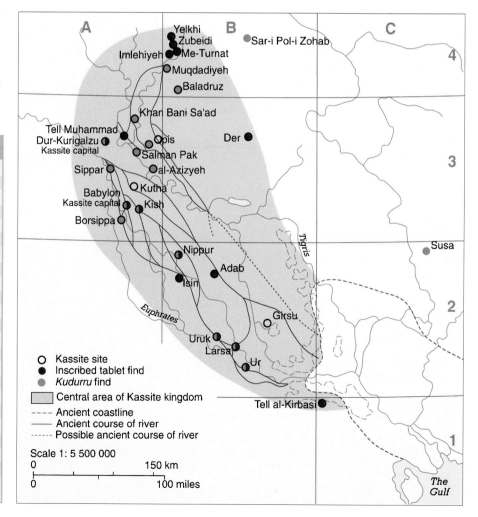

Kassite site ○
Inscribed tablet find ●
Kudurru find ●
Central area of Kassite kingdom
---- Ancient coastline
—— Ancient course of river
····· Possible ancient course of river

Scale 1: 5 500 000
0 — 150 km
0 — 100 miles

▲ Made from limestone, this *kudurru*, or boundary stone, is beautifully carved. Boundary stones were often used to record the granting of areas of land.

▶ The ziggurat of Dur-Kurigalzu. European travelers thought that the ziggurat was the Tower of Babel. The reed matting laid between every seven layers of brick can still be seen. The bottom platform is a modern restoration.

▼ This painted pottery head, found at Dur-Kurigalzu, shows the realism of Kassite art. The man's face is painted with red ocher, and his beard and other features are in black.

Kassite art and culture

The Kassites kept the Babylonian way of life, even rebuilding the temples of the Mesopotamian gods, who were different from theirs. Their art was lively and realistic, especially when it depicted animals. Their scribes left thousands of documents that were written on clay tablets.

They were the first people in West Asia to make molded baked bricks to form decorative wall friezes. At the Inanna temple at Uruk, the outer wall shows the gods as humans. Molded baked bricks were used 1,000 years later in the palaces built by Nebuchadrezzar at Babylon and by Darius at Susa.

The Kassites also showed skill in carving stone. Boundary stones (*kudurru*) were set up to proclaim when land was given to individuals by royal grants. They were often richly decorated with images of beasts that symbolized the gods who were believed to witness such grants. *Kudurrus* are the only artworks that survive from the Kassite period.

Kassite kings

Several Kassite kings are named in the Amarna letters. Burna-Buriash II (1359–1333 B.C.E.) is recorded as complaining that the Egyptian delegation who came to collect his daughter and take her to Egypt to be married had only five carriages—not enough for a princess of high rank. The Amarna letters detail the many gifts that were exchanged between the Kassite king and the Egyptian pharaoh. The Kassite king Kurigalzu I (about 1390) received gold from Egypt.

The most famous king was Kurigalzu II (1332–1308 B.C.E.), who was a successful military leader. He attacked the Elamites and captured Susa, their capital city, where inscriptions bearing his name have been found. Later the tables were turned when the Elamite king Shutruk-Nahhunte attacked the Kassite kingdom. Babylon, the capital, was destroyed and much booty was taken back to Susa. The Kassite period ended in 1154 B.C.E.

Everyday Life

B Y ABOUT 2000 B.C.E. MOST PEOPLE IN West Asia lived in towns and cities that were protected by walls. Houses were made of mud-brick and had two stories with flat roofs. The doors and windows were made from reeds set in wooden frames. The streets were narrow and winding, and resembled the old parts of cities in the region today.

Food and drink

Barley was used for bread flour and for beermaking. Beer was also brewed from dates, which were an important source of sugar, since honey was rare. Of beer it was said, "it makes the liver happy and fills the heart with joy." People grew onions, garlic, figs, and pomegranates. Mustard, cress, cumin, and coriander were used. Sheep, goats, and pigs provided meat, and people also bred ducks and geese for food. There were many different types of fish. Locusts were considered a delicacy.

Clothing and textiles

Cloth was made from the fleece of sheep, which was spun on hand-spindles. Spinning and weaving were done mainly by women, who worked in the home to provide a source of household income. Hides of animals were tanned to make leather goods such as bags and sandals.

Men and women used both soap and cosmetics. They painted the skin around their eyes with kohl, a metal-based black paint.

Town crafts

There were many different occupations in the towns. Potters produced a wide range of household items, from plates and cups to large containers used for storing grain. Carpenters made wooden furniture and tools, though these were also made from copper, tin, and bronze. Other craftworkers manufactured metal and glass objects, but these were luxury items and not used by ordinary people.

▶ This 4.5-in- (11-cm-) high sieve pot may have been used to strain the grains when pouring beer, a very popular drink. Pottery items made in a wide variety of shapes and sizes are the most commonly found objects of ancient daily life.

▶ A West Asian street market. In the shadow of the ziggurat, traders sell their wares from small booths. The jars hold imported olive oil and wine, while dates and a variety of spices are also on sale. A temple official checks the quality of the food being sold. Because coins were not invented until the seventh century B.C.E., payment was made in corn, measured using standard weights that were often carved in the shape of animals or birds, especially ducks.

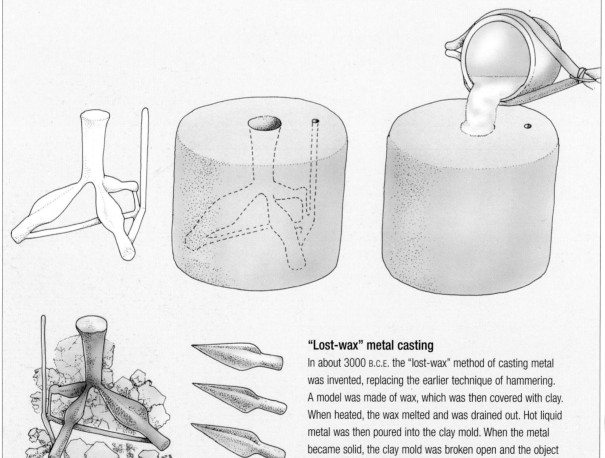

"Lost-wax" metal casting

In about 3000 B.C.E. the "lost-wax" method of casting metal was invented, replacing the earlier technique of hammering. A model was made of wax, which was then covered with clay. When heated, the wax melted and was drained out. Hot liquid metal was then poured into the clay mold. When the metal became solid, the clay mold was broken open and the object was taken out. This method was used for a wide variety of objects, from arrowheads to life-size sculptures.

New Powers

IN ABOUT 1200 B.C.E. SMALL GROUPS OF raiders emerged in West Asia and the Levant. The great Hittite empire crumbled, and Egypt was severely shaken. New political forces arose to shape the history of West Asia for the next 1,000 years and more.

The Sea Peoples

Egypt and the Levant were attacked by seafaring raiders known as the "Sea Peoples." Pharaoh Ramesses III (1194–1163 B.C.E.) fought these invaders, who were probably made up of several different tribal groups. The Sea Peoples may have come from the Aegean in the west.

One of the seafaring tribes, driven out of Egypt by Ramesses III, settled on the Mediterranean coastal plains. These people were called the Philistines in the Bible, and their name lives on in the modern word Palestine. The Philistines adopted much of the local Canaanite culture, but their distinctive decorated pottery shows that they must have had contact with Mycenaean (Greek) cultures.

Babylon and Assyria

Babylon remained under the rule of local kings. Its power grew again briefly under Nebuchadrezzar I (1126–1105 B.C.E.). He plundered the neighboring capital Susa, bringing back to Babylon the statue of Marduk that had been looted by the Elamite king Shutruk-Nahhunte in 1159 B.C.E.

Assyria became a great power when Tiglath-Pileser I (1115–1077 B.C.E.) expanded its territories as far as the Levant. His campaigns against such peoples as the Ahlamu, or Aramaeans, were recorded in graphic detail on stone carvings at his palace in Nineveh. These carvings depict shocking war scenes. Tiglath-Pileser I also hunted wild elephants in northern Syria.

The Aramaeans

The Aramaeans were originally nomads who came from the Syrian desert. They established several small kingdoms in northern Syria and the Levant, blocking Assyria's advance to the Mediterranean. Aramaean power grew, and Adad-apla-iddina (1069–1048 B.C.E.), king of Babylon, was called the "Aramaean usurper." The Aramaeans spoke Aramaic, which replaced Akkadian as the main language of West Asia until Arabic emerged in 700 C.E. Aramaic continues to be spoken in villages in Syria, Kurdistan, and northern Iraq.

▲ The triumph of the Egyptian pharaoh over his enemies is symbolized in this famous ivory carving, which was looted from the Iraq Museum and has not been recovered.

▼ The infantry troops of Tiglath-Pileser I (1115–1077 B.C.E.) are laying siege to a city in Syria. Its gates are firmly shut, but its walls are being breached by a movable wooden siege-engine that is manned from the inside and carries archers on top. The city's defending soldiers have leather-and-wicker shields. Their weapons are made from bronze, although iron was sometimes used at this time.

◀ A decorated thirteenth-century-B.C.E. pot from Ugarit, Syria. Similar vessels have been found in Cyprus.

◀ Female clay figurines from about 900 B.C.E., found near the coast of the Levant. They represent the goddess Astarte and emphasize fertility.

▲ Modern Gaza on the coast of Israel. In the twelfth and eleventh centuries B.C.E., it was the center of Philistine power and a gateway to Egypt along the coast. In the Bible, it is where Samson met his death.

Kings of Egypt, Assyria, and Babylonia

Egypt
1194–1163 B.C.E. Pharaoh Ramesses III

Assyria
1115–1066 B.C.E. Tiglath-Pileser I

Babylonia (Second Dynasty of Isin)
1126–1105 B.C.E. Nebuchadrezzar I
1069–1048 B.C.E. Adad-apla-iddina

Elam
c.1159 B.C.E. Shutruk-Nahhunte

▶ The Assyrian empire of Tiglath-Pileser I. The empire extended to the western Euphrates and was not troubled by the Sea Peoples who overran Egypt, the Levant, and Anatolia.

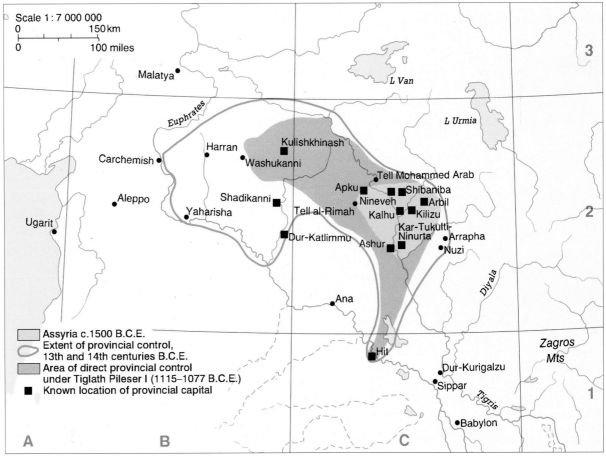

Scale 1 : 7 000 000
0   150km
0   100 miles

Malatya
L Van
L Urmia
Euphrates
Kulishkhinash
Harran
Washukanni
Carchemish
Tell Mohammed Arab
Apku
Shibaniba
Aleppo
Shadikanni
Nineveh
Arbil
Yaharisha
Tell al-Rimah
Kalhu
Kilizu
Ugarit
Dur-Katlimmu
Kar-Tukulti-Ninurta
Arrapha
Ashur
Nuzi
Diyala
Ana
Hit
Zagros Mts
Dur-Kurigalzu
Sippar
Tigris
Babylon

☐ Assyria c.1500 B.C.E.
⬭ Extent of provincial control, 13th and 14th centuries B.C.E.
▨ Area of direct provincial control under Tiglath Pileser I (1115–1077 B.C.E.)
■ Known location of provincial capital

A   B   C

Israel and Judah

PHARAOH MERNEPTAH'S VICTORY STELE boasted in 1229 B.C.E. that "Israel is laid waste." He was referring to another people who had recently emerged in West Asia, rather than to an area of land.

The Bible and Israelite history

How the Israelites settled in the land of Canaan is recorded in the Bible. The book of Exodus describes their departure from Egypt and the wanderings of the 12 tribes in the Sinai peninsula region. The books of Joshua and Judges tell how the Israelites tried to settle in Canaan. They met with stiff resistance from the local inhabitants and the Philistines who lived on the rich coastal plain.

In about 1080 B.C.E. the Philistines tried to expand their control over the hill country where the Israelite tribes had settled. Faced by this threat, the loosely knit tribes united under the leadership of Saul, the first king of Israel. The two books of Samuel report the development of the Israelite monarchy.

King David

David was a brilliant king (as well as a warrior, musician, and poet). He was installed as a vassal at Hebron in Judah by the Philistines. Hebron then became the first capital of King David's kingdom. In 995 B.C.E. David threw off the Philistine overlordship and captured Jerusalem, the capital of the Jebusites, a Canaanite tribe.

David made Jerusalem his royal city. It was well placed to control his kingdom, which united Judah in the south with Israel in the north. David also made Jerusalem the religious center of the Israelite nation, bringing there the Ark of the Covenant (the sacred container of the scrolls of Jewish law) that the Philistines had captured earlier.

The Kingdom of Israel and Judah

David, 1000–962 B.C.E.
Reigns seven years at Hebron, 33 years at Jerusalem, but these periods partly overlap

995 B.C.E. David establishes capital at Jerusalem

Solomon, 962–922 (?) B.C.E.
The date given for Solomon's death varies from 935 to 928 or 922 B.C.E., depending on the system of calculation used

▼ The united kingdom of Israel and Judah. Jerusalem was made the capital city by King David and made splendid by his son, King Solomon. When Solomon died, the kingdom divided into Israel in the north and Judah in the south. In 924 B.C.E. the Egyptian pharaoh Shoshenq invaded, but the two kingdoms survived intact until the late eighth century B.C.E.

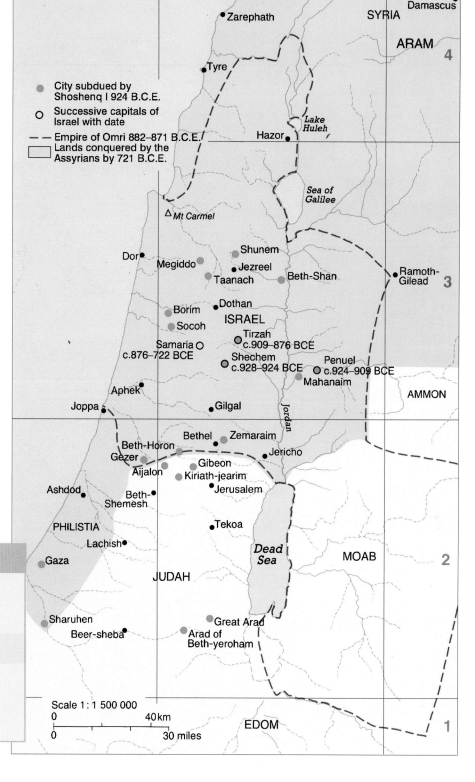

Solomon's achievements

King Solomon, David's son, built the temple in Jerusalem to house the sacred Ark of the Covenant. The Muslim Dome of the Rock now occupies the same site. No trace of Solomon's building has been found, but descriptions are given in the Bible (1 Kings, chapters 5–8, and 2 Chronicles, chapters 2–7). The temple built by Herod the Great, in which Jesus walked, was built centuries later.

Solomon also built a palace, using luxury materials, such as ivory and beams of cedar and cypress wood. The design of his palace and the temple was influenced by styles from Phoenicia, the cosmopolitan northern neighbor of the united kingdom of Israel and Judah.

Outside Jerusalem, there is more archaeological evidence of Solomon's building activities. Triple-chambered city gates that he had erected have been found at Megiddo, Hazor, and Gezer. At Megiddo there were stables for hundreds of horses. Solomon's large army used horse-drawn chariots. At Ezion-Gezer on the Gulf of Aqaba, Solomon had an industrial complex for smelting copper. At this port Solomon also built a fleet of ships to trade on the Red Sea with east Africa and Arabia.

▲ The Dome of the Rock is built over the rock where, according to tradition, Abraham was about to sacrifice Isaac, his only son. The beautiful shrine was completed in 691 C.E. and in medieval times was thought to be the center of the world.

▶ Solomon's Temple in Jerusalem. The plan of the building resembled Phoenician architecture. It was rectangular, with a porch flanked by a pair of bronze columns called Jachin and Boaz. The Holy Place was paneled in cedar wood. Only the high priest could enter the Holy of Holies through its double doors. In the temple forecourt a huge bronze basin with water stood supported by 12 bronze bulls. This basin was used for rituals.

Mesopotamian Sites

Kalhu

THE CITY OF KALHU IS IN NORTHERN IRAQ, at the join of the Tigris and Great Zab rivers, south of Mosul. The site is also called Nimrud. Kalhu became important when the Assyrian king Ashurnasirpal II (883–859 B.C.E.) selected it as his capital city. It remained the capital of Assyria for more than 150 years. Shalmaneser III (858–824 B.C.E.) also built a palace there. Kalhu is mentioned in the Bible (Genesis, chapter 10), as Calah.

Ashurnasirpal's city

By 878 B.C.E., after Ashurnasirpal II had decided to move his capital from Ashur, a major building program began at Kalhu. A canal was dug from the Great Zab River to provide water. The city was enclosed in massive walls 5 miles (8 km) long that took 70 million bricks to build. Kalhu occupied 900 acres (360 ha) and included a ziggurat and temples as well as a magnificent palace.

Ashurnasirpal was very proud of his new capital. An inscription at Kalhu describes a great feast, or banquet, that was held to celebrate the completion of the Northwest Palace. The feasting lasted 10 days, and there were 69,574 guests from all parts of the Assyrian empire.

▼ The Northwest Palace at Kalhu. Around the outer courtyard were offices. The throne room was used for official functions. The king's private quarters were around the inner courtyard.

▲ One of the ivory chairbacks that was found in a storage room at Fort Shalmaneser. It was probably made in northern Syria. The Assyrian kings' furniture was often decorated with ivory.

▼ How the throne room in the Northwest Palace might have looked—an artist's impression. Colored murals were set above the stone panels, and human-headed lions guarded the entrance.

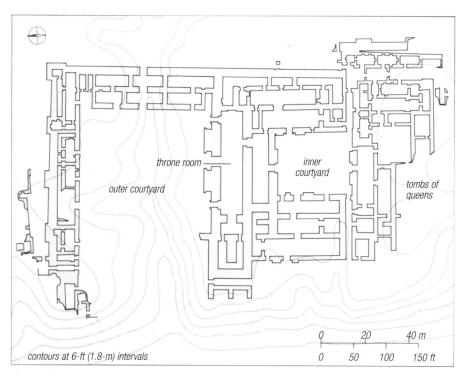

throne room

inner courtyard

outer courtyard

tombs of queens

0   20   40 m

contours at 6-ft (1.8-m) intervals

0   50   100   150 ft

Kalhu's sculptures

Excavations at the city of Kalhu produced some remarkable discoveries. Carved stone panels decorated the courtyard walls and the adjoining throne room of the Northwest Palace. They recorded the king at war and hunting, and fulfilling his religious duties. Ashurnasirpal is also shown receiving gifts, including monkeys, from foreigners. The reliefs, which were once brightly painted, also record in fine detail the fabrics, clothes, and jewelry of the king and his officials.

Treasures of Kalhu

Kings and courtiers were buried in vaulted chamber tombs. Three tombs of Assyrian queens were excavated at Kalhu, and their treasures were discovered intact. The magnificent gold jewelry has survived the destruction of both Gulf Wars.

Thousands of carved ivory fragments were found at an arsenal and in a well. Many pieces had been war booty collected by the Assyrians during their campaigns in the Levant and hidden for safekeeping when the Medes sacked Kalhu in 612 B.C.E.

► One of the treasures found in the royal tombs at Kalhu. This gold wristlet was set with a precious agate stone and inlaid with enamel. Gold winged genies hold buckets and pinecones. The wall reliefs at Kalhu depict the kings wearing wristlets similar to this one.

Late Assyrian Rule (1000–750 B.C.E.)

AFTER BEING WEAKENED FOR SEVERAL centuries by the raids of the Aramaeans, the Assyrians grew powerful again in about 900 B.C.E. Adad-nirari II (911–891 B.C.E.) defeated Babylonia and seized control of the Khabur region in the east. His son Tukulti-Ninurta II (890–884 B.C.E.) and his grandson Ashurnasirpal II (883–859 B.C.E.) continued his military successes.

Ashurnasirpal II went to war every year and gained a reputation for great brutality. Although his claim to be always victorious was probably untrue, in 877 B.C.E. he reached the Mediterranean without opposition. He called it "the Great Sea of the land Amurru."

Ashurnasirpal received much tribute from the rich Phoenician states, including "gold, silver, tin, bronze, a bronze cauldron, linen garments with multicolored trimmings, a large female ape and a small female ape, ebony, boxwood, ivory, and sea creatures."

He probably used some of these items in the construction of his splendid palace at Kalhu.

▼ The Balawat gates, a pair of massive bronze-clad gates built by Shalmaneser III, found 10 miles (16 km) northeast of Kalhu. The detail (left) shows chariots with six-spoked wheels, as was the custom in the ninth century. Each "leaf" of the gates was about 6.5 ft (2 m) wide and 13 ft (4 m) high. Sixteen embossed bands of bronze were engraved with scenes from Shalmaneser's conquests, including campaigns against the Urartu, who lived in the Lake Van region of present-day Turkey.

Shalmaneser III and Ahab of Israel

Shalmaneser III (858–824 B.C.E.) brought Assyrian power to a new height. After conquering the Aramaean state of Bit Adini in 854 B.C.E., the next year he led his armies against an alliance of kings that included Ben-Hadad of Damascus and Ahab of Israel (869–850 B.C.E.). Ahab had 10,000 foot soldiers and 2,000 chariots.

Shalmaneser was the first Assyrian ruler to come into contact with an Israelite king. After the battle, at Qarqar on the Orontes River, he erected the Black Obelisk (a tall stone monument) at Kalhu and inscribed on it his claims of an overwhelming victory.

The biblical account in 1 Kings, chapter 20, suggests that Shalmaneser's success was more limited, but by 838 B.C.E. most states in the region had to pay him tribute.

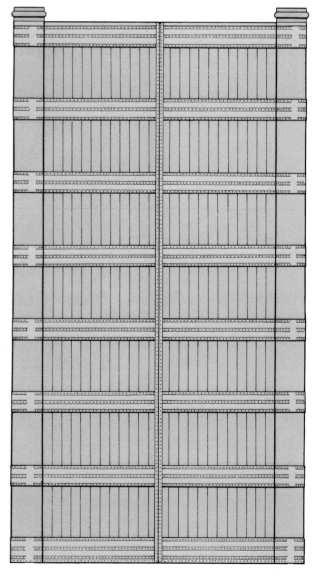

▶ Shamsi-Adad V (823–811 B.C.E.) on a stele from Kalhu. The king is in his court robes and is wearing the Assyrian royal headdress and diadem.

▼ Detail from the Black Obelisk of Shalmaneser III (858–824 B.C.E.). The cuneiform inscription identifies the man on his knees kissing the ground before the king as the Israelite king Jehu. The camels were tribute from Egypt.

Friendship with Babylon, then war

In 851 B.C.E. Shalmaneser III helped the king of Babylon defeat a revolt against him. The two kings regarded each other as equals and allies. A throne base found at Kalhu shows both men clasping hands. Shalmaneser III respected Babylonian religion and visited the temples of Marduk at Babylon and Nabu at Borsippa. He also gave the local citizens gifts and held banquets for them. This was unusual, because the Assyrian king usually demanded vast amounts of tribute.

By the time of Shamshi-Adad V (823–811 B.C.E.), the alliance with Babylon was over, and war broke out between the two kingdoms.

Assyria Triumphant (750–626 B.C.E.)

STRONG KINGS TOOK THE ASSYRIAN empire to the peak of its power between 750 and 626 B.C.E. They are mentioned in the Bible (2 Kings).

Tiglath-Pileser III

Tiglath-Pileser III (744–727 B.C.E.) was a successful ruler. He reorganized the army and replaced vassal kings with loyal provincial governors. He introduced a "royal mail" service—his messengers traveled in chariots drawn by mules to all parts of the empire. Tiglath-Pileser III also deported many of the people he conquered to curb future rebellions.

Shalmaneser V (726–722 B.C.E.) succeeded his father. Records of his short reign have not survived, but the Bible (2 Kings, chapter 17, verses 3–6) tells how he captured Israel when King Hosea rebelled. Shalmaneser V may have died during the three-year siege of Samaria.

▼ The Assyrian empire in the late eighth century B.C.E. The capital city of the empire was Ashur in northern Mesopotamia. The lands controlled by the Assyrians extended from Ur near the Gulf and included the kingdom of Israel. Jerusalem and the kingdom of Judah only came under their control between 733 and 650 B.C.E. An efficient road system linked the distant parts of the empire, with travelers' rest-houses at regular intervals along the highways.

Sargon II

How Sargon II (722–705 B.C.E.) came to be king is unknown, but he was a capable leader. At Qarqar on the Orontes River, Sargon defeated an alliance of Syrian states, establishing Assyrian control as far as Egypt. In Asia Minor he controlled the Phrygians, whose king was the legendary Midas. In 714 B.C.E. he destroyed Musasir, capital of the Urartu. The kings of Cyprus paid tribute to him. In 709 B.C.E. Sargon became king of Babylon, ruling West Asia from the Gulf to the Sinai desert. Sargon was killed in a minor clash in 705 B.C.E. His body was lost so he could not be buried in his palace.

Kings of Assyria 744–626 B.C.E.
744–727 B.C.E. Tiglath-Pileser III
726–722 B.C.E. Shalmaneser V
722–705 B.C.E. Sargon II
704–681 B.C.E. Sennacherib
680–669 B.C.E. Esarhaddon
668–626 B.C.E. Ashurbanipal

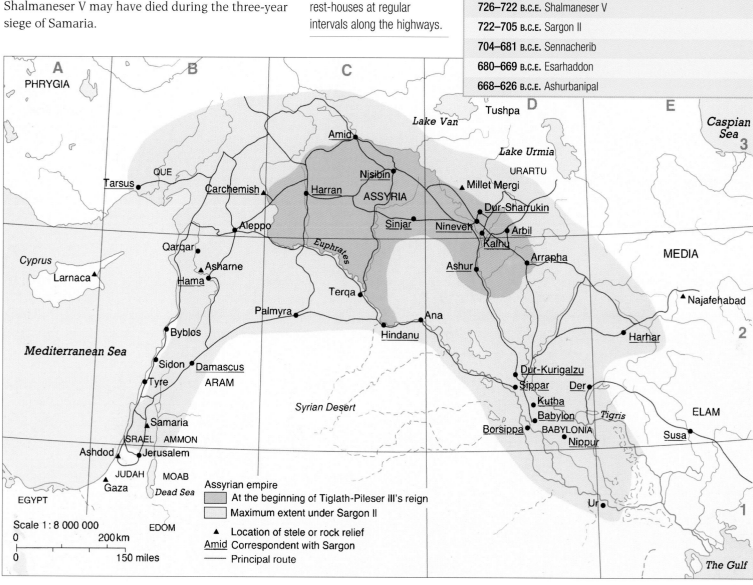

Scale 1 : 8 000 000
0 — 200 km
0 — 150 miles

Assyrian empire
- At the beginning of Tiglath-Pileser III's reign
- Maximum extent under Sargon II
- ▲ Location of stele or rock relief
- <u>Amid</u> Correspondent with Sargon
- —— Principal route

Sargon's successors

Sennacherib (704–681 B.C.E.) was Sargon's son. His capture of Lachish in 701 B.C.E. and his dealings with Hezekiah, king of Judah, are recorded in the Bible (2 Kings, chapter 18) and in a dramatic frieze that is now in the British Museum. Problems with Babylon occupied Sennacherib until 694 B.C.E., when he destroyed the city. One of his own sons then murdered him. Esarhaddon (680–669 B.C.E.), Sargon's crown prince, claimed the throne. He captured Memphis from the Egyptians in 671 B.C.E., but died on a second campaign in 669 B.C.E.

Esarhaddon's two crown princes succeeded him. Ashurbanipal, king of Assyria, overshadowed his brother, king of Babylon, both as a military leader and as a man of learning. Ashurbanipal collected many cuneiform texts from all over his empire for his famous library at Nineveh.

◀ A stone carving recording one of the campaigns of the Assyrian kings. Here an Assyrian soldier is shown cutting off the head of the Elamite king whom Ashurbanipal defeated in 635 B.C.E.

▼ A royal procession enters Babylon through the Ishtar gate. It was over 46 ft (14 m) high and made of blue-glazed bricks that were decorated with bulls and dragons. The king rides in his chariot, sheltered by an umbrella, the symbol of royalty. The first chariot carries his senior court official.

Mesopotamian Sites

Ashur

ASHUR LIES ON A ROCKY OUTCROP OF LAND overlooking the Tigris River in northern Iraq. It had been an outpost of southern influence from about 2300 B.C.E. Sumerian-style statues from the Early Dynastic period and inscriptions were found here.

City of trade

Ashur was situated on an important trade route to Anatolia, where in about 2000 B.C.E. merchants from the city established a trading colony at Kanesh. Donkey caravans carried woolen textiles and tin that had been mined in Iran to Ashur, from where they were distributed farther afield. Many cuneiform tablets discovered at Kanesh show that a lively correspondence went on between the two depots.

Assyrian capital

Although Ashur was well placed for trade, it was not an obvious site for the capital of a kingdom, because of the lack of farmland surrounding it. Despite this, the Middle and Late Assyrian rulers favored the city.

Adad-nirari I (1305–1274 B.C.E.) built a large palace at Ashur. Tukulti-Ninurta I (1243–1207 B.C.E.) dug a moat around the western side of the city, which was open to attack. He also rebuilt the Ishtar temple and started work on a new palace.

Ashur kept its reputation as a religious center even after Ashurnasirpal II (883–859 B.C.E.) shifted his capital to Kalhu. There was a ziggurat and many temples, apart from the major shrine to Ashur, the city god who was a combination of the Sumerian god Enlil and the Babylonian deity Marduk. The tombs of five Assyrian kings have been found at Ashur. They include those of Ashurnasirpal II and Shamsi-Adad V (823–811 B.C.E.), who built or reconstructed most of the public and religious buildings. Later Assyrian kings built three ziggurats and at least 38 temples inside the 346-acre (140-ha) city.

Between 614 and 612 B.C.E. the Medes from Iran invaded Assyria and looted Ashur. In the first and second centuries it was resettled and became known as Labbana. Recently the site was threatened by flooding from a proposed dam on the Tigris River, but this project, proposed by the deposed Iraqi leader Saddam Hussein, has now been dropped.

▲ The tomb and sarcophagus (stone coffin) of the Middle Assyrian king Ashur-belkals (1074–1057 B.C.E.), one of five royal burial places discovered at Ashur.

▼ The site of Ashur. There were many temples, including the temple of the city god, also called Ashur. The palace, the ziggurat, and the temples were sited on the steep northern cliffs overlooking the old course of the Tigris. The river now flows on the eastern side of the promontory. The western side was protected by a wall and a moat.

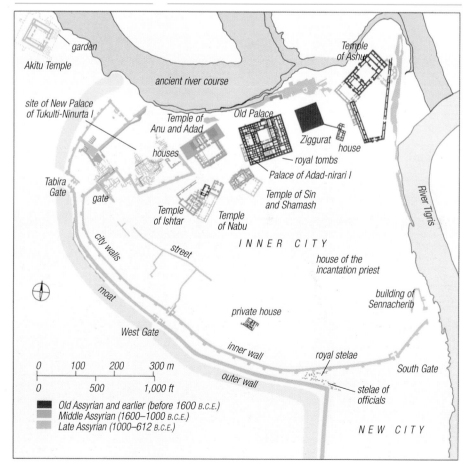

Nineveh

NINEVEH WAS ONE OF THE GREATEST cities of Mesopotamia. It is situated on the eastern side of the Tigris River near modern Mosul in northern Iraq. It stood on one of the major western trade routes between the Mediterranean and the Indian Ocean, and was therefore a wealthy city. The site was enclosed by more than 7.5 miles (12 km) of city walls and has two main mounds: Nebi Yunus (the citadel) and Kuyunjik (the arsenal).

Under the dynasty of Agade, Manishtushu (2269–2255 B.C.E.) founded the famous temple of Ishtar at Nineveh, mentioned by Hammurabi in his law code. Here was found the superb bronze life-sized head of Naram-Sin (2254–2218 B.C.E.), one of the great Mesopotamian art treasures.

The Late Assyrian ruler Sennacherib (705–681 B.C.E.) made Nineveh his capital. His Southwest Palace was decorated with carved stone reliefs showing, among other scenes, the siege and capture of Lachish. Sennacherib's grandson Ashurbanipal (669–627 B.C.E.) built the North Palace on Kuyunjik for his cuneiform library.

Genesis, chapter 10, verse 11, mentions Nineveh, and the biblical books of Nahum and Jonah prophesy the city's downfall. In 612 B.C.E. Nineveh was destroyed by the Babylonians and Medes. Its fall marked the collapse of the Assyrian empire.

▶ A reconstruction of the walls and towers at Nineveh. The mound of Nebi Yunus (the citadel) is the traditional Muslim burial site of the prophet Jonah.

▼ Ashurbanipal and his queen Ashur-sharrat feast in their gardens—possibly those of the Northwest Palace at Nineveh, where the carving was found. In the pine tree on the left hangs the head of an enemy king.

Warfare

STONE AND WOODEN TOOLS, SUCH AS arrowheads, clubs, spears, and slings used to hunt animals, became the first weapons. Weapons made of copper, including axes, spears, and daggers, were in use by about 4000 B.C.E. Bronze weapons were used about 2000 B.C.E. and iron 1,000 years later.

How early wars were fought

Armies were well organized. The Sumerian "Stele of the Vultures," dated 2450 B.C.E., shows soldiers from Lagash. The men march in military formation with their spears and axes, protected by their shields, behind their leader, Eannatum. In Sumer, the warrior-lugals, or "great men," became the first kings.

The first fortified city was Jericho, whose massive walls (they still stand 13 feet/4 m high) and a round tower 26 feet (8 m) high were built as long ago as 8000 B.C.E. As more cities constructed similar defenses, siege warfare developed as a way of capturing these places. Military machinery, such as battering rams and siege towers, came into use by about 1000 B.C.E.

Horses revolutionized war. Slow-moving carts drawn by mules had been used in Sumerian times. In about 1500 B.C.E. the first two-wheeled horse-drawn war chariots were used. Cavalry units, introduced by the Assyrians, rode bareback, because the saddle had not yet been invented.

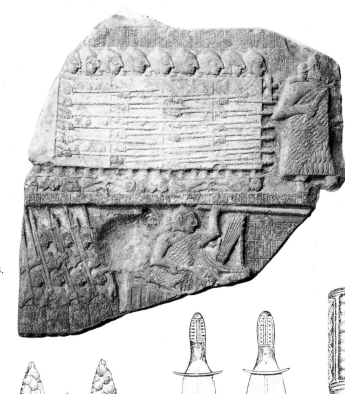

◀ The Stele of the Vultures is the first known carving showing an army at war. On the lower part of this fragment, King Eannatum rides in a chariot, followed by his foot soldiers. This may be a victory parade to celebrate the success of the war shown in the upper part of the fragment.

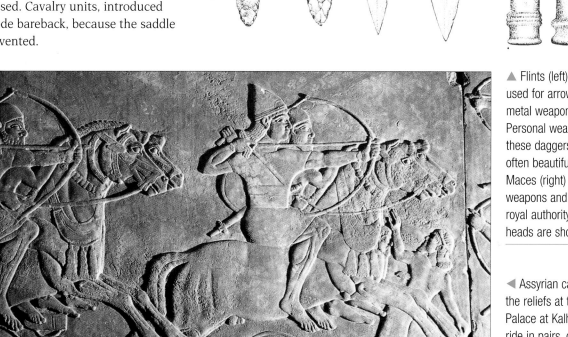

▲ Flints (left) were still used for arrowheads after metal weapons were cast. Personal weapons, such as these daggers (middle), were often beautifully decorated. Maces (right) were both weapons and symbols of royal authority—just the heads are shown here.

◀ Assyrian cavalrymen from the reliefs at the Northwest Palace at Kalhu. The men ride in pairs, one steering the horses, and the other shooting with bow and arrow. Their defeated enemies lie trampled and decapitated under the horses' hooves.

▶ A crescent-shaped bronze axhead dating from about 2400 B.C.E. The axhead was fitted into a slot in the haft (wooden handle) and fastened with nails or bolts. Other axheads were cast in metal with a hole to take the haft.

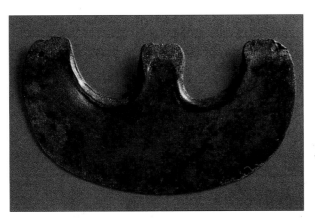

The Assyrian army

The Assyrian army was a well-developed fighting machine, with as many as 50,000 troops. It received its supplies through taxes, tribute, and war booty. Some of the soldiers were mercenaries—foreign professional soldiers who fought for money.

The king was always the commander-in-chief of the army. Provincial governors often acted as the generals. Sometimes senior palace officials also led the troops. Tiglath-Pileser III (744–727 B.C.E.) appointed his chief eunuch commander of his chariot forces. Before going into battle, kings would consult omen-tellers who would reveal the will of the gods.

The infantry

The infantry, or foot soldiers, were a large and important part of the Assyrian army. The men came from the poorer families or were slaves sent by their wealthy owners.

The light infantry uniform was a short tunic, a cone-shaped helmet, and a lightweight shield made of wicker and leather. The heavy infantry uniform was a long robe covered with metal plates. This was one of the earliest forms of chain mail and made a weighty load. The weapons of the infantryman included a sling (for throwing stones), a longbow, and a pike.

It was the job of the infantry to force its way through holes broken in the walls of cities being besieged. Archers were positioned in the top of assault towers, which were made of wicker and leather on a wooden frame. The towers were wheeled and were equipped with battering rams.

Chariot warfare

Fewer in number than the infantry, the chariot troops of the Assyrian army were usually highborn Assyrians. They were the army's elite. Chariots were manned by a charioteer and an archer, sometimes protected by two shield-bearers.

Chariots were drawn by two horses, sometimes with a third horse not yoked to the chariot but kept as a spare to replace an exhausted beast in battle. A tablet from Amarna includes the words "I have sent ... precious stones, 15 pairs of horses for five wooden chariots."

The body of the chariots was square and probably made of wickerwork, with the wheel axle at the back end. Chariots were open at the back. Spears, the battle ax, and other weapons were kept in a box attached to the front.

▼ The art of war in Assyrian times. The bronze panels of the Balawat gates show scenes from the wars fought by the Assyrians. Here an Assyrian siege-engine, with archers on top, attacks a city in northern Syria. Siege warfare was an important part of the Assyrians' method of conquest and is depicted in their reliefs.

▼ This detail from the Balawat gates shows Phoenician boats bringing tribute from the island of Tyre to the mainland for Shalmaneser III. Both the Assyrians and, later, the Persians used the famous Phoenician navy in warfare.

◀ An Assyrian war chariot, from the Balawat gates. Shalmaneser III's chariot forces were the elite of his army. Chariots were also used for hunting and in ceremonial processions. In the late eighth century B.C.E. cavalry grew in importance, especially for fighting in the mountains, where chariots could not go.

Babylonian Revival (626–560 B.C.E.)

THE LATE ASSYRIAN PERIOD WAS A troubled time for Babylon, which had 24 kings between 900 and 681 B.C.E. The city's fortunes changed when Esarhaddon (680–669 B.C.E.) became king. By the end of the next century Babylon became rich, powerful, and famous.

Nabopolassar

Nabopolassar (625–605 B.C.E.), who claimed to be the "son of a nobody," founded the New Babylonian dynasty. After 10 years of fighting the Assyrians in the Babylonian territories, Nabopolassar gained enough power to march north. He intended to attack Ashur, the religious capital of the Assyrians.

Before Nabopolassar could strike, Ashur was overrun by the Medes, from northwest Iran. The Babylonian and Median armies joined forces and in 612 B.C.E. they captured Nineveh after a three-month siege, looting the palaces and temples.

In 1990 a tangled mass of skeletons was excavated at the Halzi gate—grim evidence of Nineveh's population trying to flee the invaders. Some were heavily armed and must have been slain as they attempted to defend the city.

Neo-Babylonian Kings	
The Chaldean dynasty, 625–562 B.C.E.	
625–605 B.C.E.	**Nabopolassar**
614 B.C.E.	Destruction of Ashur
612 B.C.E.	Sack of Nineveh
605–562 B.C.E.	**Nebuchadrezzar**
605 B.C.E.	Defeat of Pharaoh Necho at Carchemish, in Syria

Kings of Judah, 640–587 B.C.E.	
640–609 B.C.E.	Josiah
	Josiah takes advantage of Assyria's weakness to reestablish the Davidic kingdom but is killed in 609 B.C.E. by Pharaoh Necho II at Megiddo
609–598 B.C.E.	Jehoiakim
598–597 B.C.E.	Jehoiachin
597 B.C.E.	Jehoiachin deported to Babylon
597–587 B.C.E.	Zedekiah
587 B.C.E.	Siege of Jerusalem, destruction of the temple, deportation of citizens to Babylon

▼ Nebuchadrezzar and his wife relax in the beautiful Hanging Gardens of Babylon. They are being fanned by servants and entertained by a court musician playing a harp. The king and queen wear embroidered garments decorated with sequins made of gold. They are enjoying drinks chilled with ice from the royal icehouse. An icehouse was found at the palace of Zimri-Lim at Mari dating from about 2000 B.C.E.

▲ The Ishtar gate, built of blue glazed bricks, was taken from Babylon and is in the Pergamon Museum, Berlin. The gate originally stood between the outer and inner walls of the city of Babylon. The processional way ran from it to the sacred area of the city. The great processions that took place during the 11-day Akitu, or New Year festival, would have passed through the gate. The bulls and dragons on the gate are made from molded baked bricks. Bulls were the symbol of Adad, god of thunder. Dragons were the symbols of Marduk, the city god of Babylon.

Nebuchadrezzar

Before he became king, Nebuchadrezzar, Nabopolassar's son and crown prince, had tasted success in battle. In 605 B.C.E. he defeated the Egyptian pharaoh Necho at Carchemish in northern Syria. He left the kingdom of Judah alone, because King Jehoiakim had paid him tribute. On the death of his father in 605 B.C.E., Nebuchadrezzar returned to Babylon to be crowned king. He had marched for three weeks, covering more than 30 miles (48 km) a day, to return for his coronation.

Babylon and the Jews

Jehoiakim (609–598 B.C.E.) succeeded his father Josiah (640–609 B.C.E.) as king of Judah. He accepted Nebuchadrezzar as his overlord. Then, in 601–600 B.C.E. Jehoiakim rebelled. Nebuchadrezzar captured Jerusalem in 597 B.C.E. He took Judah's new king, Jehoiachin, the son of Jehoiakim, and his mother, wives, and officials in chains to Babylon.

Nebuchadrezzar appointed Jehoiachin's uncle, Zedekiah (597–587 B.C.E.), king of Judah. But

Zedekiah also rebelled. The Babylonians laid siege to Jerusalem, and broke through its defenses in 587–586 B.C.E. They destroyed much of the city, deporting the Jewish population to Babylon and carrying away treasures from the temple. The Bible records these events in the books of 2 Kings, 2 Chronicles, Jeremiah, and David.

Nebuchadrezzar's great city

Nebuchadrezzar was responsible for rebuilding the city and restoring Babylon's wealth and reputation. He took a leading role in the great 10-day Akitu festival, marking the Babylonian New Year.

He carried out massive rebuilding programs at the temple of Marduk and the ziggurat, as well as constructing the fabled Hanging Gardens for one of his wives, who was homesick for the mountains of her native Media. Nebuchadrezzar also surrounded Babylon with walls that encircled an area of more than 3 square miles (8 sq. km). The excavations of Robert Koldewey in the late nineteenth century revealed much of the Late Babylonian city.

▲ This black stone tablet has an inscription recording the rebuilding of Babylon and its temples by Esarhaddon (the city's king from 680 to 669 B.C.E.). It shows the Assyrian king holding his mace, the symbol of royal power, and standing respectfully before a temple. Just behind him is the sacred tree of life and the bull, symbol of the god of thunder. The plow below suggests the agricultural and economic wealth that Esarhaddon succeeded in restoring to Babylon.

79

Mesopotamian Sites

Babylon

"BABYLON SURPASSES IN SPLENDOR ANY city of the known world," wrote the Greek historian Herodotus, who visited Babylon in about 450 B.C.E. The site is about 50 miles south of Baghdad, in present-day Iraq. The city became important under Hammurabi (1792–1750 B.C.E.). But it resisted Assyrian rule and was destroyed by Sennacherib (705–681 B.C.E.).

In the Neo-Babylonian period, Babylon was capital of the empire. Nebopolassar and his son Nebuchadrezzar (605–562 B.C.E.) carried out a huge building program. The city remained important under the later Persian rulers, opening its gates to Cyrus in 539 B.C.E. The Persian kings then made Babylon their winter residence.

Alexander the Great also entered the city without resistance. After Alexander's death at Babylon, his general Seleucus built a new capital farther along the Tigris River, and Babylon sank into decline.

"Gates of the gods"

The name Babylon means "gate of the gods." The site was roughly rectangular and had a double wall of defense. The main route across the city was the processional way. Entry to the city was through eight gateways, each protected by a god or goddess. The most spectacular was the gate dedicated to Ishtar, with its brilliant blue glazed bricks decorated with bulls and dragons.

The Hanging Gardens

Ancient historians rated the Hanging Gardens of Babylon as one of the Seven Wonders of the World. Nebuchadrezzar built them for his homesick wife, but the site of the famous gardens has not been found. Nor has that of the famous Tower of Babel mentioned in the Bible. This reference, in Genesis, chapter 11, probably was to the ziggurat, which was called Etemenanki.

▼ Ancient Babylon covered an area of over 2,150 acres (70 ha)—larger than many modern towns. At the time of Nebuchadrezzar, the Euphrates River flowed through the city, dividing it into two sections, which were connected by a bridge. In the older, eastern part (left) was the king's palace, near the Ishtar gate (bottom left). From here the processional way led toward the great temple of Marduk and the ziggurat (top center). The western part of Babylon (right) was probably a residential area.

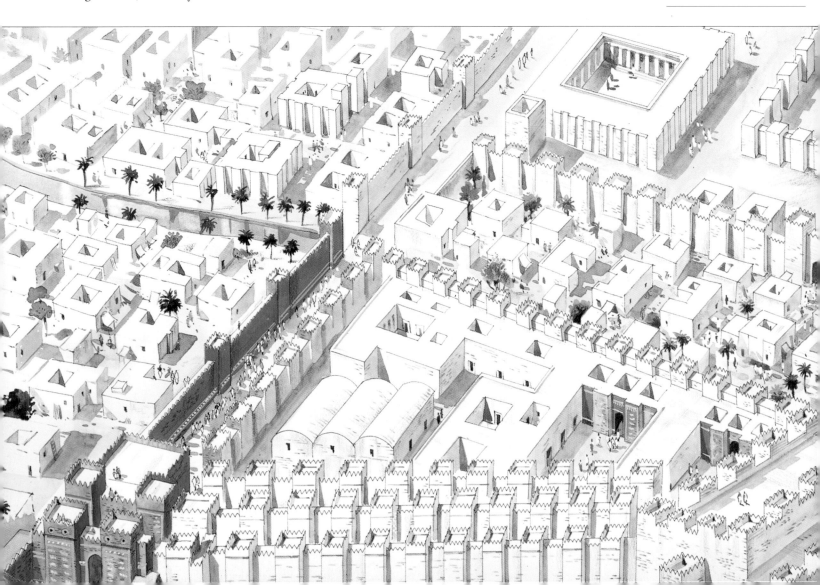

◀ A glazed relief brick panel from Darius' palace at Susa. The winged lion has ram's horns and is decorated in blues and greens. Embossed colored tiles developed because of the lack of stone in the region.

▲ Basalt statue of the lion of Babylon trampling a man beneath him. This was found in the ruins of the Northern Palace, which was built by Nebuchadrezzar. It was part of a "museum" belonging to the king.

The Persian Empire (560–521 B.C.E.)

CYRUS BECAME KING OF THE PERSIANS in 559 B.C.E. The Median king Astyges was his overlord. Other rulers of the time were Croesus of Lydia and Nabonidus of Babylon. Cyrus conquered all three kings and founded the Persian empire, which dominated West Asia for the next 200 years.

The conquests of Cyrus (559–530 B.C.E.)

In 550 B.C.E. Cyrus turned against Astyges, king of the Medes. The Medes had overrun the cities of Ashur, Kalhu, and Nineveh in 612–614 B.C.E., ending the Assyrian dynasty. Now Cyrus marched to the Median capital at Hamadan, emptied the treasury, and took possession of vast lands stretching from Turkey to Central Asia.

In 547 B.C.E. Cyrus led his armies to the western borders of his empire to do battle with the Lydians. Croesus, the Lydian king, was legendary for his wealth. Gold was abundant in his lands, and the Lydians may have been the first people to use large numbers of coins, which were stamped to guarantee their quality and their weight.

Croesus' territories included the Greek cities of the Aegean coast. When Croesus heard of Cyrus'

defeat of the Medes, he thought he could expand his empire. He consulted the oracle at Delphi before going to war and learned that a great empire would be destroyed. Croesus did not realize that the empire to be destroyed was his—at the hands of Cyrus.

Babylon: jewel in Cyrus' crown

The Babylonian king Nabonidus (555–539 B.C.E.) was more than 60 years old when he came to the throne. He rebuilt the temple to the moon god Sin in Harran and installed his daughter as the priestess of Sin at Ur. This was a time of poverty, plague, and famine in Babylon.

For unknown reasons, Nabonidus left Babylon to live in Taima, in northwest Arabia. He left his son Belshazzar to rule in his place and, because there was no king, the Akitu, or New Year's festival, could not be celebrated for 10 years. This was considered to be a bad omen.

Nabonidus was unpopular with the people of Babylon because he had neglected the religion of the city's god, Marduk. In 539 B.C.E. the Akitu festival was celebrated, and was described by the Greek historians and in the biblical book of Daniel, but the end of the Babylonian dynasty had arrived.

▼ The growth of the Persian empire. Cyrus' vast lands stretched from the coast of the Mediterranean to the Indus valley. The Persians had been ruled by the Medes when Cyrus became king. Within a few years he had conquered the territories of the Medes, which stretched to Central Asia in the east, the Babylonian lands in the south, and the Lydian kingdom, in modern Turkey, in the west. Cyrus' son Cambyses also controlled Egypt.

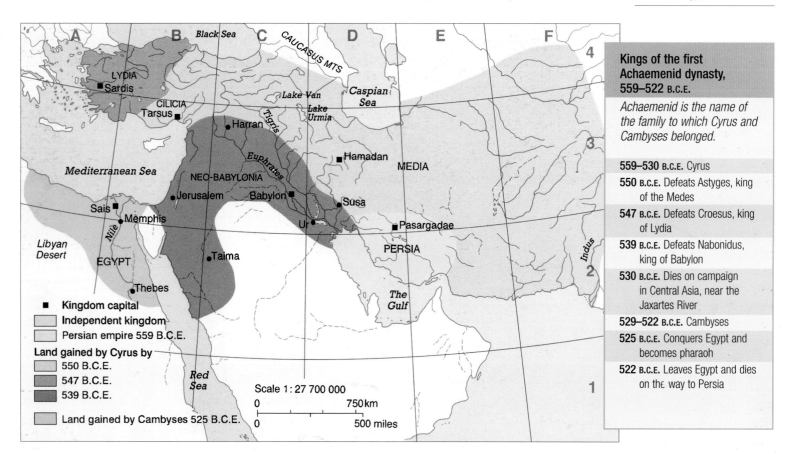

Kings of the first Achaemenid dynasty, 559–522 B.C.E.

Achaemenid is the name of the family to which Cyrus and Cambyses belonged.

559–530 B.C.E. Cyrus

550 B.C.E. Defeats Astyges, king of the Medes

547 B.C.E. Defeats Croesus, king of Lydia

539 B.C.E. Defeats Nabonidus, king of Babylon

530 B.C.E. Dies on campaign in Central Asia, near the Jaxartes River

529–522 B.C.E. Cambyses

525 B.C.E. Conquers Egypt and becomes pharaoh

522 B.C.E. Leaves Egypt and dies on the way to Persia

Map legend:

- ■ Kingdom capital
- Independent kingdom
- Persian empire 559 B.C.E.
- Land gained by Cyrus by
  - 550 B.C.E.
  - 547 B.C.E.
  - 539 B.C.E.
- Land gained by Cambyses 525 B.C.E.

Scale 1 : 27 700 000
0 — 750km
0 — 500 miles

Cyrus arrived with his army at Babylon in 539 B.C.E. and entered the city without a battle. The Babylonians did not resist. Many of them, celebrating a religious festival, did not even know about his arrival. Cyrus told his troops not to damage the city or its temples.

Foundation of the Persian empire

Cyrus proclaimed himself "king of the world, great king ... king of Babylon, king of Sumer and Akkad." The Greek historians considered him a benevolent conqueror and a model ruler. He allowed the Jews who had been exiled in Babylon by Nebuchadrezzar to return to Jerusalem and rebuild the temple, as related in the biblical book of Ezra.

Cyrus used Lydian craftsmen to build his capital at Pasargadae, in modern Iran. Work started in about 546 B.C.E. He was buried there in 530 B.C.E. after being killed in battle in Central Asia.

Cyrus' son, Cambyses (529–522 B.C.E.), expanded the empire to include Egypt, which he conquered in 525 B.C.E. Cambyses had the reputation of being a tyrant. He lived in Egypt and acted like a pharaoh. In 522 B.C.E. he left Egypt to return to Persia but he died on the way.

▲ Cyrus had his own tomb built at Pasargadae, his capital. It is a simple gabled building set on a stepped platform. An inscription on the tomb reads: "I am Cyrus, who founded the empire of the Persians and was king of Asia. Grudge me not therefore this monument."

▶ Remains of a palace at Pasargadae. The city's palaces were inspired by Median architecture and are not like those in Mesopotamia. They had columned halls and open porticoes that allowed access to the beautiful gardens in which they were set. Lydian stonemasons may have made the columns, which are similar to ones found at Ephesus in western Turkey.

Darius' Empire (521–486 B.C.E.)

DARIUS (521–486 B.C.E.) RULED THE Persian empire after Cambyses. Under his brilliant rule, the empire reached into Europe, but Darius had come to the throne only after a considerable struggle.

The Behistun inscription

In the famous inscription of Behistun, Darius told the world about his fight to become king after Cambyses died in 522 B.C.E. Carved on a rock about 300 feet (100 m) off the ground, overlooking the main caravan route from Babylon to Hamadan in northern Iran, the inscription is in three languages: Old Persian, Babylonian, and Elamite.

Darius claimed that after Cambyses murdered his own brother, Bardiya, before setting out to Egypt, a

▼ Building materials for the palace at Susa. Darius made the city of Susa the capital of his huge empire. He imported materials from every corner of his territories to build his palace there. In 500 B.C.E. he built a canal from the Nile River to the Red Sea, making it much easier to bring goods by ship from Egypt. Darius was proud of the resources used and left inscriptions at Susa listing the people and the materials involved in building his palace.

priest called Gaumata seized the throne. He pretended to be Bardiya and was accepted as king. Nobody dared resist Gaumata until Darius killed him in 522 B.C.E.

The real truth is probably that Darius took the Persian throne by force from Cambyses' brother. Darius did belong to the Achaemenid family, after which the dynasty is named, but he was not in direct line to the throne.

Rebellions broke out in many parts of the Persian empire after Cambyses died. Within a year Darius had established his rule over the kings of Persia, Elam, Media, Assyria, Egypt, Parthia, Margian, Sattagydia, and Scythia.

This achievement is recorded on the relief that accompanies the Behistun inscription. The carving

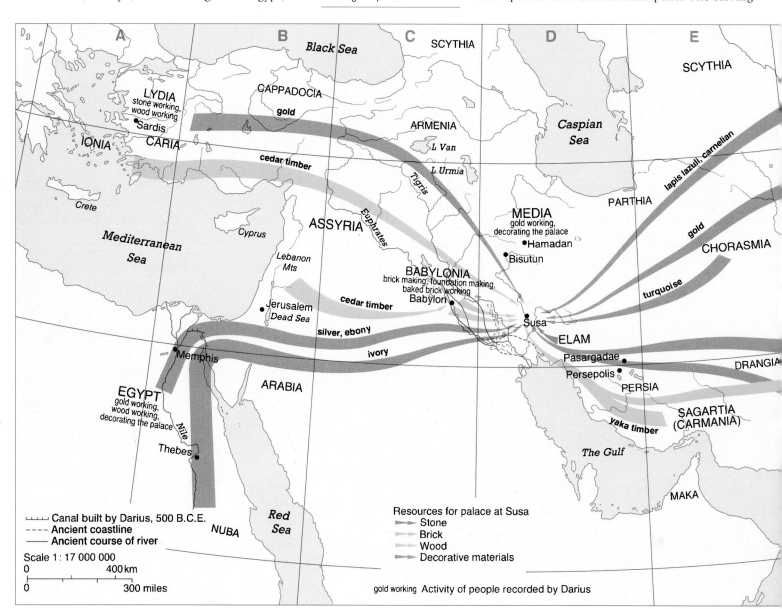

Canal built by Darius, 500 B.C.E.
Ancient coastline
Ancient course of river

Scale 1 : 17 000 000
0   400 km
0   300 miles

Resources for palace at Susa
Stone
Brick
Wood
Decorative materials

gold working Activity of people recorded by Darius

shows Darius beneath the winged standard of Ahura-Mazda, the great god of the Zoroastrian religion, receiving the homage of his conquered peoples, represented by nine kings.

Darius was a Zoroastrian and believed that he had been chosen to rule by the supreme god, Ahura-Mazda. He thought that kingship was a gift from the gods and that kings therefore had special responsibilities to their people.

At Naqsh-i Rastam, where Darius was buried in a rock-cut tomb, an inscription proclaimed that Darius had been made king by Ahura-Mazda; he was a friend to good and an enemy to evil; he protected the weak from the strong and also the strong from the weak; he desired what was right; he was a good horseman, a good archer, and a good spearman.

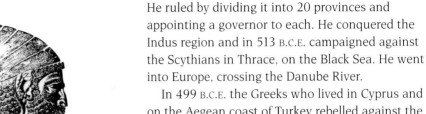

The Persian empire under Darius

Darius' empire reached from Central Asia to Egypt. He ruled by dividing it into 20 provinces and appointing a governor to each. He conquered the Indus region and in 513 B.C.E. campaigned against the Scythians in Thrace, on the Black Sea. He went into Europe, crossing the Danube River.

In 499 B.C.E. the Greeks who lived in Cyprus and on the Aegean coast of Turkey rebelled against the Persians. The Ionian revolt lasted for six years. Darius used the Phoenician navy to regain Cyprus, but the Greek cities on the Turkish coast were much harder to control.

In 494 B.C.E. a naval battle took place off the island of Lade, near Miletus. The Persian fleet of 600 ships overwhelmed the much smaller Greek navy. Darius now turned his attention to mainland Greece, but the Greeks finally defeated the Persian army at Marathon in 490 B.C.E.

Darius died in 486 B.C.E. His son Xerxes inherited a very well-organized empire, with a regular taxation system and efficient communications. Like the Assyrians before them, the Persians relied on a fast horseback messenger service with relay stations providing fresh mounts.

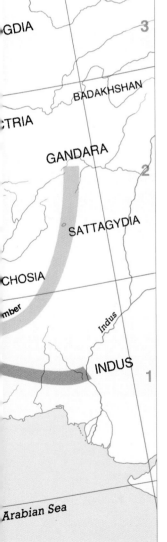

▼ This molded and glazed brick panel from Susa, from the twelfth century B.C.E., was thrown away by Darius. This form of ornamental brickwork was first produced by the Kassites in Mesopotamia, then used by the Persians.

▲ Darius was king over many nations. Delegations brought gifts to him, as shown in this stone carving. The Bactrian (from Bactria in Central Asia) holds a pair of bracelets similar to some found in Afghanistan today.

Sites

Susa

SUSA IS SITUATED ON THE PLAINS OF Khuzestan in southwest Iran. In about 2500 B.C.E. the city was the capital of Elam, which had links with the Fars region and with Anshan to the southeast. With the rise of the dynasty of Agade in 2300 B.C.E., Susa came under Mesopotamian control. In 2004 B.C.E. it was reunited with Anshan, beginning the Elamite era. Almost 800 years later, in one of the most brilliant periods of their history, the Elamites overran Mesopotamia and brought its finest art treasures as war booty to Susa.

Ashurbanipal (668–627 B.C.E.) captured Susa and completely destroyed it. He sowed the fields with salt so that no crops could grow—an ancient method of chemical warfare.

◀ A glazed brick relief from Darius' palace at Susa. The archer was probably one of the king's bodyguards. This decorated brickwork may have been made by Mesopotamian workers who were brought to Susa.

▼ The fronts of two bulls placed together made the column capitals (topmost parts) for the palace at Susa. A heavy wooden beam rested on the animals' backs.

◀ This gold statue of a man with a kid is one of a pair. The other is made from silver. Both statues were probably gifts of thanks made by a private person to the temple at Susa. They are not Persian but from an earlier period, about 1100 B.C.E.

▼ The site of Susa, which was identified in 1851, has four mounds. Three of them—the palace, the acropolis or "high place," which was the main religious center, and the royal city— belong to the period of the Persian empire.

City of Darius

The time of the Persian empire was a golden period for Susa. The city blossomed under Darius the Great (522–486 B.C.E.), who made it his administrative capital. On the Apadana mound of the city he built a large palace, combining Babylonian and Median architecture. Workers and luxury materials were brought from all parts of the Persian empire, including cedar wood from the Lebanon Mountains.

Darius' palace at Susa is mentioned in the biblical books of Esther and Nehemiah, where the city is called Shushan.

Alexander the Great captured Susa in 331 B.C.E. To cement his empire together, he arranged the mass marriage of Greek soldiers and Persian women there. Marked by an unusual white stone cone, the tomb of the biblical prophet Daniel is thought to be near the acropolis area (now the village of Shush) and is still visited by Muslim pilgrims.

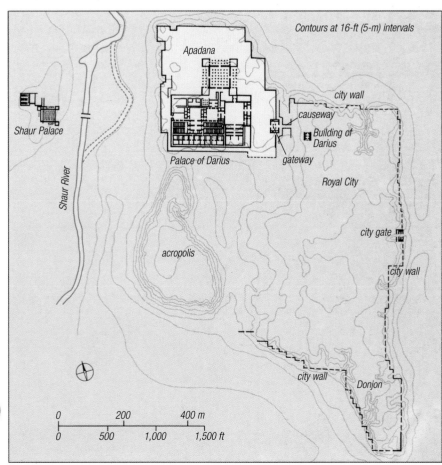

The Final Years (486–323 B.C.E.)

THE LAST YEARS OF THE PERSIAN EMPIRE were a time of struggle with the Greeks. The Persians gained some early victories, but they were followed by defeats.

Xerxes against the Greeks

Darius' son Xerxes (486–465 B.C.E.) was his chosen successor. According to Herodotus, the Greek historian, Xerxes led 2 million men against Greece in 480 B.C.E. He captured Athens, but the Greek navy defeated the Persian fleet at the battle of Salamis. Xerxes returned to Persia, leaving his general Mardonius in command. After an indecisive land battle at Plataia in 479 B.C.E., the Persian armies left Greece, but the Persian fleet was again defeated, this time at Mycale in Ionia.

Murder in the Persian court

Despite the Greek defeats, the Persian empire remained intact until Xerxes died, or was perhaps killed by three of his courtiers, in 465 B.C.E. Now the Persian court entered a period of plots and multiple murders, often by poisoning. One of Xerxes' sons killed another. Then, in 425 B.C.E., three of Xerxes' grandsons ruled in quick succession, the first two being murdered after only a few months on the throne. More royal conspiracies and murders followed for almost 100 years.

Darius III and Alexander

Darius III (335–330 B.C.E.) had survived all the palace plots. But in 334 B.C.E. a greater problem arose. Alexander of Macedon, known as Alexander the Great, led his army against the Persian empire. Alexander's troops defeated those of Darius time after time, and in 331 B.C.E., near Babylon, Darius fled the battlefield, only to be killed by his courtiers.

Alexander took command of the entire Persian empire. He now ruled the great cities of Babylon, Susa, Persepolis, and Hamadan. The empire of Cyrus and Darius, which had survived for 150 years, was at an end, and so was the great civilization of ancient West Asia.

◀ A procession of the soldiers of all nations lines the stairway at Persepolis leading to the Apadana palace. Darius I began to build the city of Persepolis. His son Xerxes continued the work, and his grandson Artaxerxes completed it.

▶ The empire of Alexander the Great. When Alexander defeated Darius III at Gaugamela in 331 B.C.E., he became lord of all the Persian territories, which extended to Central Asia and India. When he died at the age of 33, his generals divided up the vast kingdom between them. West Asia went to Seleucus, and Egypt was governed by Ptolemy.

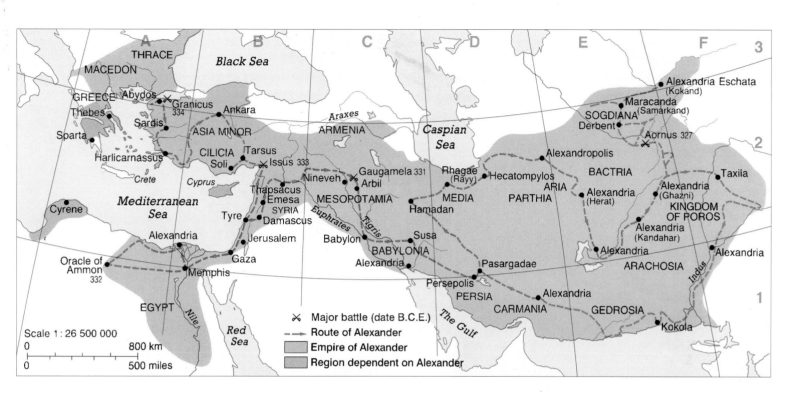

Scale 1 : 26 500 000

✕	Major battle (date B.C.E.)
---→	Route of Alexander
	Empire of Alexander
	Region dependent on Alexander

▶ The main reception hall of the Apadana palace at Persepolis. Here the king would receive important foreign visitors. The columns are almost 66 ft (20m) high and have ornate capitals in the shape of bulls or lions. Columned halls were typical of Persian architecture.

◀ Alexander the Great (356–323 B.C.E.) leads his armies on a campaign. His conquests stretched from Macedonia and Greece to the Indus River in Asia. In battle against the Indian king Porhates, Alexander crossed the Indus. His army defeated the Indians, whose elephants panicked in battle. But Alexander's Greek troops were homesick, so he began the long march back to Greece. Reaching Babylon in 323 B.C.E., Alexander, the invincible warrior, caught a fever and soon died.

War and Looting

BOOTY WAS PART OF WAR IN ANCIENT West Asia. In 1159 B.C.E. the Elamites sacked Babylon, taking the sacred treasures of the Mesopotamians. They seized the stele of Naram-Sin, Hammurabi's law code, and statues of Nanna from Uruk and Marduk from Babylon. Some of these priceless treasures were never returned and were discovered, by chance, at Susa during the last century. Antiquities (objects from ancient times) command high prices. In 1880 three merchants were robbed in Afghanistan of their gold treasure. The thieves were found, and the Oxus treasure, named after the river where it was discovered, was given to the British Museum.

Gold objects are highly sought after, because they are easily sold or simply melted down into bars. The gold treasure from the royal tombs at Kalhu was put in a bank vault in Baghdad during the 1990–91 Gulf War. Trade in stolen or illegal objects is highly profitable and is on the increase. In several countries, including Afghanistan and Iraq, many famous sites resemble lunar landscapes—they have been totally destroyed by looters looking for treasure to sell on the international antiquities market.

▶ One of more than 1,500 objects in the Oxus treasure, which dates from the Persian empire. A gold sheet showing a man, probably a priest, wearing tight trousers and tunic. This style of clothing was worn by Persians when hunting or in battle.

▼ From the Oxus treasure. A gold roundel (sequin) that would have been sewn onto a garment. The clothing of Persian and Assyrian kings was often decorated in this way, as can be seen in the carved reliefs at Kalhu.

War damage in West Asia

The 1980–88 Iran–Iraq War, the 1990–91 Gulf War, and the Gulf War of 2003 caused great damage to the ancient monuments of Mesopotamia. The ziggurat built by Ur-Nammu at Ur and the Northwest Palace of Ashurnasirpal at Nineveh, for example, suffered direct hits. The extent of damage will not be known for a long time. Site exploration is severely limited owing to the danger of unexploded landmines and bombs in southern Iraq, which is home to the great cities of Uruk, Eridu, and Ur, among others.

Looting and the illegal antiquities trade

In the 1990–91 Gulf War many provincial museums in Iraq were looted. Most of the terra-cotta figurines, cuneiform tablets, and other artifacts have not been recovered. The 2003 looting of the Iraq Museum in Baghdad grabbed world attention. Some objects have been recovered, but many priceless items are still missing. Following the 2003 Gulf War, the illegal excavation of archaeological sites has been the greatest threat. Much money is made from the sale of such illegally acquired items—the proceeds are often used to finance insurgency and terrorist activities.

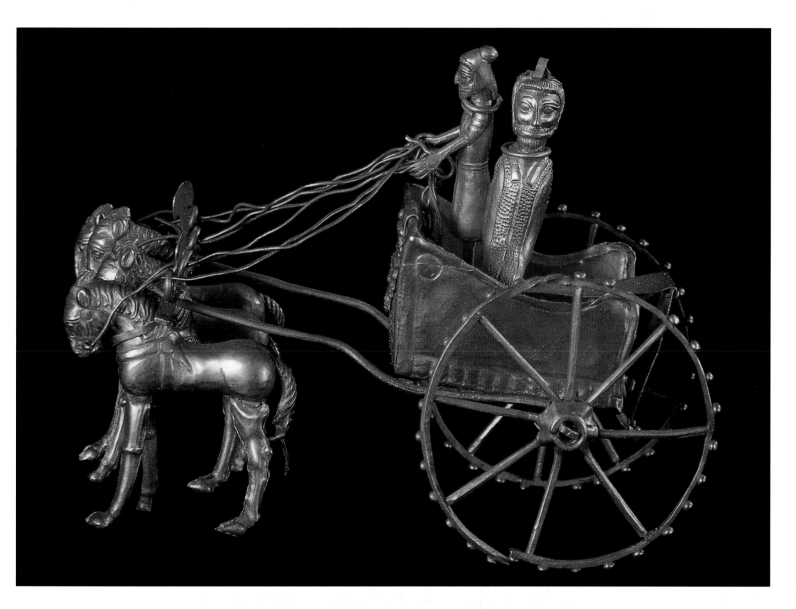

▲ A gold model of a chariot from the Oxus treasure. The chariot is drawn by four horses and has on the front a head like that of the Egyptian god Bes. The model is less than 8 in (20 cm) long.

◄ This gold armlet from the Oxus treasure is in the British Museum, London. The hollow spaces would have been filled with colored enamels. The bracelet must have been a popular design, since a similar one is shown in the stone carvings at Persepolis as part of the Bactrian tribute. The gold jewelry from the royal tombs at Kalhu is equally beautiful.

Glossary

Aceramic A term given to the Neolithic period (c.8500–7000 B.C.E.) before pottery was invented.

Akkad The northern part of Mesopotamia. The southern area was called Sumer. Akkad was named after the city Agade, but by about 1800 B.C.E. the region was called Babylonia.

Akkadian The dynasty founded by Sargon (c.2300 B.C.E.). Also the name of a Semitic language that was spoken in Mesopotamia as early as 3000 B.C.E.

Anatolia The highland plains of present-day central Turkey.

Assyria The northern part of modern Iraq, near the border with Turkey.

Assyrian A dialect of Akkadian spoken by the Assyrians. Also the name of a dynasty that has three main periods (c.2000–612 B.C.E.).

Babylonia The region of southern Mesopotamia that was called Akkad before about 1800 B.C.E.

Babylonian A dialect of Akkadian spoken by Babylonians. Also the name of the dynasty that ruled from about 2000 B.C.E. to 750 B.C.E.

cuneiform The wedge-shaped script of Akkadian that was written on clay tablets and was used throughout Mesopotamia and the Near East.

diorite A very hard black stone that was used to make statues.

dynasty A line of rulers usually from a single family or related through marriage.

Epi-Paleolithic The continuation of the Paleolithic or Old Stone Age culture after the last Ice Age. This period, which is sometimes called the Mesolithic, was followed by the Neolithic period.

Fertile Crescent The lands between the highland zones of Turkey and Iran and the deserts of Arabia, having 8 inches (20 cm) of rainfall each year.

figurine A small statue made from wood, ivory, clay, or metal.

flint A hard stone used to make tools in the Paleolithic, Epi-Paleolithic, and Neolithic periods.

king list A list of the names of kings and the lengths of their reigns. The best known is the Sumerian King List, which records the dynasties ruling the cities of Sumer until 2000 B.C.E.

lapis lazuli A semiprecious blue stone that is found only in the mountains of Afghanistan.

law code A collection of laws recording the penalties for different crimes. The best-known law code is that of Hammurabi (c.1800 B.C.E.).

Levant The lands bordering the eastern Mediterranean, now modern Lebanon, Israel, and coastal Syria.

Mesolithic The Middle Stone Age period between the Paleolithic, or Old Stone Age and the Neolithic, or New Stone Age. Also known as the Epi-Paleolithic.

Mesopotamia A Greek word meaning "between the rivers" and describing the lands in present-day Iraq, from south of modern Baghdad to the Persian Gulf. The northern part of Mesopotamia was called Akkad, the southern lands Sumer.

microliths Very small chipped stone tools that first appear in the Mesolithic period.

Natufian A culture of the Epi-Paleolithic period in the Levant (c.11,000–9300 B.C.E.) when people began to grow grain.

Neolithic The New Stone Age (c.9300–4000 B.C.E.), which was divided into the Proto-Neolithic and Aceramic periods.

obsidian A natural volcanic glass from Anatolia that is much sharper than flint and was used to make tools.

Paleolithic The Old Stone Age, which ended with the last Ice Age in about 12,000 B.C.E. People obtained their food by hunting and gathering during this period.

pharaoh The title of the king of ancient Egypt.

Proto-Neolithic The period during the New Stone Age when grain was first grown (c.9000–8500 B.C.E.).

Semitic The language family that was widely spoken in Mesopotamia and the Near East and includes Akkadian and its dialects, Assyrian and Babylonian.

stele An upright stone or wooden slab, often decorated with carvings or bearing inscriptions.

Sumer The southern lands of Mesopotamia, reaching the Persian Gulf, that were occupied by the Sumerians. The plain north of modern Baghdad was called Akkad.

Sumerian The language that was spoken in Sumer by the Sumerians in about 4000 B.C.E. Sumerian does not belong to the Semitic language family.

tablet A small flat slab, usually made of clay, on which an inscription in cuneiform would be written.

tell An Arabic word for a mound made by the remains of ancient settlements. Often part of a place name, as in Tell Madhhur.

ziggurat A high tower built in stepped stages with a temple at the top.

FURTHER READING

Bahrani, Z. *Women of Babylon: Gender and Representation in Mesopotamia* (Routledge, 2001).
Charvet, P. *Mesopotamia Before History* (Routledge, 2002).
Collon, D. *Ancient Near Eastern Art* (British Museum Press, 1995).
Crawford, H. *Sumer and the Sumerians* (Cambridge University Press, 2004).
Curtis, J. *Ancient Persia* (British Museum Press, 2000).
Gurney, O. R. *The Hittites* (Viking Penguin, 1991).
Leick, G. *Mesopotamia: The Invention of the City* (Penguin, 2000).
Matthews, R. *The Archaeology of Mesopotamia: Theories and Approaches* (Routledge, 2003).
Nicolle, D. *History of Medieval Life* (Chancellor Press, 1997).
Oates, J. C. *Babylon* (Thames & Hudson, 1986).
Perce, A. *Art of the Ancient Near East* (Harry N. Abrams, 1980).
Pollock, S. *Ancient Mesopotamia* (Cambridge University Press, 1999).
Roaf, M. *Cultural Atlas of Mesopotamia and the Ancient Near East* (Facts On File, 1990).
Roux, G. *Ancient Iraq* (Viking Penguin, 1993).

Schuster, A. M. M., and M. Polk (eds.). *The Looting of the Iraq Museum: The Lost Legacy of Mesopotamia* (Harry N. Abrams, 2005).
Tubb, J. *Bible Lands* (Dorling Kindersley, 1991).

Useful Web sites
http://www.crystalinks.com/mesopotamia.html
Sections on climate, government, history, language, art, and religion.

http://www.etana.org/abzu
Web site of the Oriental Institute, University of Chicago, that provides search facilities for information on the study of the ancient Near East.

http://www.iranchamber.com/history/achaemenids/achaemenids.php
Achaemenid history and culture from the Iran Chamber Society.

http://www.mesopotamia.co.uk
British Museum Web site coverage of the history and culture of ancient Mesopotamia.

Gazetteer

The gazetteer lists places and features, such as rivers or mountains, found on the maps. Each has a separate entry including a page and grid reference number. For example:
Abu Gosh 20 B2

Where a place also has an alternative name form, this name is added to the entry before the page number. For example:
Alexandria (Ghazni) 89 E2

All features are shown in italic type. For example:
Anshan, d. 52 C2

A letter after the feature describes the kind of feature:
d. district; *f.* feature;
i. island; *mt.* mountain;
mts. mountains; *r.* river

Abu Gosh 20 B2
Abu Hureyra 20 C3
Abu Salabikh 32 A3, 41 C2
Abu Salem 20 B2
Abydos 89 A3
Adab 41 C2, 47, 54 B2, 56 C2, 60 B2
Agade 52 B3, 56 C2
Aijalon 66 B2
Ain Ghazal 20 B2
Ain Mallaha 20 B2
Ain Gev I 20 B2
Akkad, d. 41 C2, 52 C3
Akshak 41 C2
al-Azizyeh 60 A3
al-Khiam 20 B2
Al-Untash-Napirisha (Choga Zanbil) 47
Alalakh 58 B2
Aleppo 58 B2, 65 B2, 72 B3
Alexandria 89 B2
Alexandria 89 C2
Alexandria 89 D1
Alexandria 89 E2
Alexandria 89 F1
Alexandria (Ghazni) 89 E2
Alexandria (Herat) 89 E2
Alexandria (Kandahar) 89 E2
Alexandria Eschata (Kokand) 89 F3
Alexandropolis 89 D2
Ali Kosh 20 E2, 29 E1
Alps, mts. 14 H6
Amanus Mts. 41 A3
Amid 72 C3
Ammon, d. 66 C3, 72 B2
Amu Darya, r. 11 G3, 14 F3
An Nafud, f. 11 C1

Ana 65 C2, 72 C2
Anatolia, d. 10 B3, 14 B3, 20 A3, 25 B3
Ankara 89 B3
Anshan, d. 52 C2
Aornus 89 E2
Apamea 29 B2
Aphek 66 A3
Apku 47, 65 C2
Arabia, d. 11 D1, 14 C1, 84 B1
Arachosia, d. 85 F2, 89 E1
Arad of Beth-yeroham 66 B2
Aram, d. 66 C4, 72 B2
Araxes, r. 89 C3
Arbil 47, 58 D2, 65 C2, 72 D3, 89 C2
Aria, d. 85 F2, 89 E2
Armanum 52 A3
Armenia, d. 84 C3, 89 C2
Arpachiyeh 29 D2
Arrapha 65 C2, 72 D2
Arslantepe 29 C3
Asharne 72 B2
Ashdod 66 A2, 72 B1
Ashikli Huyuk 20 A4
Ashkelon 29 B1
Ashur 41 C3, 47, 52 B3, 56 B3, 58 D2, 65 C2, 72 D2
Asia Minor, d. 89 B2
Assyria, d. 72 C3, 84 C2
Awan 41 D2

Babylon 47, 52 B3, 54 A3, 56 C2, 58 D1, 60 A3, 65 C1, 72 D2, 82 C3, 84 C2, 89 C2
Babylonia, d. 72 D2, 84 C2, 89 C2
Bactria, d. 85 F2, 89 E2
Bad-tibira 41 C2, 54 C2
Badakhshan, d. 85 G2
Baghouz 29 C2
Baladruz 60 B4
Balikh, r. 52 B3
Basta 20 B2
Beer-sheba 66 A2
Beidha 20 B2
Beisamoun 20 B2
Belbasi 20 A3
Beth-Horon 66 B2
Beth-Shan 66 B3
Beth-Shemesh 66 A2
Bethel 66 B2
Bisutun 84 D2
Black Sea 11 C3, 14 B3, 15 F6, 25 B3, 82 B4, 84 B3, 89 B3
Borim 66 B3
Borsippa 47, 54 A3, 56 C2, 60 A3, 72 D2
Bouqras 20 C3
Byblos 29 B2, 41 A3, 58 B2, 72 B2

Cafer Huyuk 20 C4
Can Hasan 20 A3
Cappadocia, d. 84 B3
Carchemish 58 B2, 65 B2, 72 B3
Caria, d. 84 A2
Carmania, d. 84 E1, 89 D1
Carmel, Mt. 20 B2, 66 B3
Caspian Sea 11 E3, 14 D3, 15 G6, 20 E4, 25 D3, 29 E3, 41 E3, 52 C4, 72 E3, 82 D4, 84 D3, 89 D2
Caucasus Mts. 11 D3, 82 C4
Cedar Mt. 52 A3
Chagar Bazar 29 C2
Chatal Hüyük 29 A2
Chayonu 20 C4
Choga Bonut 20 E2
Choga Mami 29 D1
Choga Zanbil *see* Al-Untash-Napirisha
Chorasmia, d. 85 E2
Cilicia, d. 82 B3, 89 B2
Crete, i. 84 A2, 89 A2
Cyprus, i. 10 B2, 20 A3, 25 A2, 29 A2, 52 A3, 72 A2, 84 B2, 89 B2
Cyrene 89 A2

Damascus 66 C4, 72 B2, 89 B2
Dasht-e Kavir, f. 11 E2
Dasht-e Lut, f. 11 F2
Dead Sea 15 F6, 29 B1, 41 A2, 52 A1, 58 B1, 66 B2, 72 B1, 84 B2
Deh-i No 47
Der 41 C2, 60 B3, 72 D2
Derbent 89 C2
Dilbat 54 A3, 56 C2
Dilmun, d. 52 C2
Diyala, r. 41 C3, 58 D2, 65 C2
Dor 66 A3
Dothan 66 B3
Drangiana, d. 84 E1
Dur-Katlimmu 65 B2
Dur-Kurigalzu 47, 60 A3, 65 C1, 72 D2
Dur-Sharrukin (Khorsabad) 47, 72 D3

Ebla 41 A3, 52 A3, 58 B2
Edom, d. 66 B1, 72 B1
Egypt, d. 10 B1, 14 B1, 52 A2, 72 A1, 82 B2, 84 A1, 89 A1
Elam, d. 11 E2, 41 D2, 52 C2, 72 E2, 84 D2
Elburz Mts. 11 E2
Emesa 89 B2
Emutbal, d. 56 C2
Eridu 29 E1, 41 D2, 47, 54 C1, 56 C1
Eshnunna 41 C2, 56 C2

Euphrates, r. 11 C2, 14 C2, 20 D2, 29 C2, 32 B1, 41 B3, 47, 52 B3, 54 A2, 56 B2, 58 C2, 60 A2, 65 B2, 72 C2, 82 C3, 84 C2, 89 C2

Galilee, Sea of 66 B3
Gandara, d. 85 F2
Ganj Dareh 20 E3
Gaugamela 89 C2
Gaza 66 A2, 72 B1, 89 B2
Gedrosia, d. 89 E1
Gezer 66 A2
Ghazni *see* Alexandria
Gibeon 66 B2
Gilgal 66 B3
Girsu 41 D2, 54 C2, 56 C2, 60 B2
Gobi, f. 14 J6
Godin Tepe 41 D3
Granicus 89 A3
Great Zab, r. 11 D2, 20 D3, 41 C3, 58 D2
Great Arad 66 B2
Greece, d. 89 A2
Gritille 20 C3
Gulf, The 11 E1, 14 D1, 15 B2, 20 E1, 25 D1, 41 D1, 47, 52 C2, 56 D1, 60 C1, 72 E1, 82 D2, 84 D1, 89 D1
Gutium, d. 41 C3

Habur, r. 11 C2, 20 C3, 29 C2, 41 B3, 52 B3, 58 C2
Hacilar 20 A3
Hajji Muhammad 29 D1
Hama 29 B2, 72 B2
Hamadan 82 D3, 84 D2, 89 C2
Hamazi 41 C3
Hamman 47
Hana, d. 56 B3
Haradum 56 B3
Harhar 72 E2
Harlicarnassus 89 A2
Harran 58 C2, 65 B2, 72 C3, 82 C3
Hasanlu 29 D2, 41 C3
Hatula 20 B2
Hazor 66 B4
Hecatompylos 89 D2
Hejaz, f. 11 C1
Herat *see* Alexandria
Himalayas, mts. 14 J5
Hindanu 72 C2
Hit 65 C1
Huleh, Lake 66 B4

Imleihiyeh 60 B4
Indus, d. 85 F1
Indus, r. 14 F1, 82 F2, 85 F1, 89 E1
Ionia, d. 84 A2

Isin 54 B2, 56 C2, 60 B2
Israel, d. 66 B3, 72 B2
Issus 89 B2

Jarmo 20 D3, 29 D2
Jericho 20 B2, 66 B2
Jerusalem 66 B2, 72 B1, 82 B3, 84 B2, 89 B2
Jezreel 66 B3
Joppa 66 A3
Jordan, r. 66 B3
Judah, d. 66 B2, 72 B1

Kalhu 47, 65 C2, 72 D3
Kandahar *see* Alexandria
Kar-Tukulti-Ninurta 47, 65 C2
Kara Kum, f. 11 F3
Karim Shahir 20 D3
Kebara 20 B2
Khafajeh 52 B3
Khan Bani Sa'ad 60 A3
Khorsabad *see* Dur-Sharrukin
Kilizu 65 C2
Kiriath-jearim 66 B2
Kish 41 C2, 47, 52 B3, 54 A3, 56 C2, 60 A3
Kisurra 54 B2
Kizil Irmak, r. 11 B3,14 B3, 52 A4, 58 B3
Kokand *see* Alexandria Eschata
Kokola 89 E1
Kul Tepe 29 D2
Kulishkhinash 65 B2
Kutha 54 A3, 56 C2, 60 A3, 72 D2

Lachish 66 A2
Lagash 41 D2, 52 C2, 56 C2
Larnaca 72 A2
Larsa 47, 54 B2, 56 C1, 60 B2
Lebanon Mts. 84 B2
Levant, d. 11 B2/C2, 14 B2
Libyan Desert 82 A2
Little Zab, r. 20 D3
Lower Sea 52 C2
Lydia, d. 82 A4, 84 A1

Macedon, d. 89 A3
Magan, d. 52 D1
Maka, d. 84 E1
Malatya 65 B3
Mananaim 66 B3
Maracanda (Samarkand) 89 E2
Marad 54 A3
Marashi, d. 52 C2
Mari 41 B3, 47, 52 B3, 56 B3
Mashkan-shapir 54 B3, 56 C2
Me-Turnat 60 B4

93

Media, d. 72 E2, 82 E3, 84 D2, 89 D2

Mediterranean Sea 10 B2, 14 A2, 15 F6, 20 A2, 25 A2, 29 A2, 52 A3, 58 A1, 72 A2, 82 A3, 84 A2, 89 A2

Megiddo 58 B1, 66 B3

Memphis 82 B2, 84 B1, 89 B1

Mersin 29 B2

Mesopotamia, d. 11 D2, 14 C2, 20 D3, 89 C2

Millet Mergi 72 D3

Moab, d. 66 B2, 72 B1

Muqdadiyeh 60 B4

Mureybet 20 C3

Nahal Hemar 20 B2

Najafehabad 72 E2

Nemrik 20 D3

Neo-Babylonia, d. 82 C3

Neribtum 56 C2

Nile, r. 10 B1, 14 B1, 20 A1, 82 B2, 84 B1, 89 B1

Nineveh 29 D2, 41 C3, 47, 52 B3, 58 D2, 65 C2, 72 B3, 89 C2

Nippur 32 A3, 41 C2, 47, 52 B3, 54 B3, 56 C2, 58 D1, 60 B2, 72 D2

Nisibin 72 C3

Niya, d. 58 B2

Nubia, d. 84 B1

Nuzi 41 C3, 65 C2, 58 D2

Oman, Gulf of 11 F1

Opis 60 A3

Oracle of Amman 89 A1

Orontes, r. 58 B2

Palegawra 20 D3

Palmyra 72 C2

Parthia, d. 84 D2, 89 D2

Pasargadae 82 D3, 84 D2, 89 D2

Pella 20 B2

Penuel 66 B3

Persepolis 84 D1, 89 D1

Persia, d. 14 D2, 82 D2, 84 D1, 89 D1

Philia 29 A2

Philistia 66 A2

Phrygia, d. 72 A3

Poros, Kingdom of, d. 89 F2

Qadesh 58 B2

Qarqar 72 B2

Qatar 15 B1

Qatara *see* Tell al-Rimah

Qermez Dere 20 D3

Que, d. 72 B3

Ramoth-Gilead 66 C3

Ras Shamra *see* Ugarit

Rayy *see* Rhagae

Red Sea 11 C1, 14 B1, 15 F5, 25 B1, 52 A1, 82 C1, 84 B1, 89 B1

Rhagae (Rayy) 89 D2

Rosh Zin 20 B2

Rosh Horesha 20 B2

Sagartia *see* Carmania

Sahara, f. 14 H5

Sais 82 B3

Salam Pak 60 A3

Samaria 66 B3, 72 B2

Samarkand *see* Maracanda

Samarra 29 D2

Sar-i Pol-i Zohab 60 B4

Sardis 82 A4, 84 A3, 89 A2

Sattagydia, d. 85 F2

Scythia, d. 84 C3, 85 E3

Shadikanni 65 B2

Shaduppum 56 C2

Shanidar 20 D3

Sharuhen 66 A2

Shatt al-Gharraf, r. 32 B3

Shatt al-Hilla, r. 32 A2

Shechem 66 B3

Sherihum, d. 52 D2

Shibaniba 65 C2

Shubat-Enlil 47

Shunem 66 B3

Shuruppak 41 C2

Shusharra 29 D2

Sidon 66 B4, 72 B2

Silver Mt. 52 A3

Simurrum 52 B3

Sinai d. 10 B1, 25 A1

Sinjar 72 C3

Sippar 41 C2, 47, 52 B3, 54 A4, 56 C2, 58 D1, 60 A3, 65 C1, 72 D2

Socoh 66 B3

Sogdia, d. 85 F3

Sogdiana, d. 89 E2

Soli 89 B2

South China Sea 14 J4

Sparta 89 A2

Subartu, d. 52 B3

Sudan 15 F5

Suhu, d. 56 B3

Sumer, d. 41 D2, 52 C2

Susa 41 D2, 47, 52 C3, 60 C2, 72 E2, 82 D3, 84 D2, 89 C2

Syria, d. 11 C2, 14 B2, 66 B4

Syrian Desert 11 C2, 14 C2, 41 B3, 72 C2

Taanach 66 B3

Taima 82 C2

Tarsus 29 B2, 41 A3, 58 B2, 72 B3, 82 B3, 89 B2

Taurus Mts. 10 B2

Taxila 89 F2

Tekoa 66 B2

Tell Agrab 41 C2

Tell al-Fakhariyeh *see* Washukanni

Tell al-Hawa 47

Tell al-Hayyad 32 B3

Tell al-Kirbasi 60 C1

Tell al-Rimah (Qatara) 47, 58 D2, 65 C2

Tell al-Sawwan 29 D2

Tell al Ubaid 41 D2

Tell Aswad 20 B2

Tell Aswad 20 C3

Tell Awayli 29 D1, 32 B1

Tell Brak 29 C2, 41 B3, 52 B3, 58 C2

Tell Dlehim 32 A2

Tell Halaf 29 C2

Tell Hasan 29 D2

Tell Jokha 41 C2

Tell Judeideh 29 B2

Tell Mismar 32 B1

Tell Mohammed Arab 65 C2

Tell Muhammad 56 C2, 60 A3

Tell Ramad 20 B2, 29 B1

Tell Shmid 32 B2

Tell Umm Dabaghiyeh 29 D2

Telul al-Thalathat 29 D2

Tepe Gawra 29 D2

Tepe Giyan 29 E2, 41 D3

Tepe Guran 20 E2, 29 E1

Tepe Sarab 29 E2

Terqa 72 C2

Thapsacus 89 B3

Thebes 82 B2, 84 B1, 89 A2

Thrace, d. 89 A3

Tigris, r. 11 D2, 14 C2, 20 D2, 29 D2, 32 B3, 41 C3, 47, 52 B3, 54 B3, 56 C3, 58 D2, 60 B2, 65 C1, 72 E2, 82 C3, 84 C2, 89 C2

Til Barsip 41 B3

Tirzah 66 B3

Tushpa 72 D3

Tuttul 66 B3

Tutub 41 C2, 56 C2

Tyre 66 B4, 72 B2, 89 B2

Ugarit (Ras Shamra) 20 B3, 29 B2, 58 B2, 65 A2

Umm al-Aqarib 32 B2

Umma 32 B2, 41 C2, 52 B2, 56 C2

Upper Sea 52 A3

Ur 15 G6, 29 E1, 41 D2, 47, 52 C2, 54 C1, 56 C1, 60 B2, 72 E1, 82 D3

Urartu, d. 72 D3

Urmia, Lake 14 D2, 15 G6, 20 D3, 29 D2, 41 C3, 47, 52 C3, 58 D2, 65 C2, 72 D3, 82 D3, 84 C2

Urua 52 C3

Uruk 32 B1, 41 C2, 47, 52 B2, 54 B2, 56 C2, 58 D1, 60 B2

Van, Lake 14 C3, 15 F6, 20 D4, 29 D3, 47, 52 B4, 58 D3, 65 C3, 72 D3, 82 C4, 84 C3

Wadi Hasa 20 B2

Wadi Dubai B 20 B2

Warium, d. 56 C3

Washukanni (Tell al-Fakhariyeh) 58 C2, 65 B2

Yaharisha 65 B2

Yarim Tepe I and II 29 D2

Yarmuti 52 A3

Yelkhi 60 B4

Zabalam 54 B2, 56 C2

Zagros Mountains 11 D2, 25 C2, 29 E1, 41 D2, 65 D1

Zahara 52 C3

Zarephath 66 B4

Zarzi 20 D3

Zawi Chemi Shanidar 20 D3

Zemaraim 66 B2

Zubeidi 60 B4

Index